D0940625

Fashion-ology

Dress, Body, Culture

Series Editor: **Joanne B. Eicher**, *Regents' Professor, University of Minnesota*

Books in this provocative series seek to articulate the connections between culture and dress which is defined here in its broadest possible sense as any modification or supplement to the body. Interdisciplinary in approach, the series highlights the dialogue between identity and dress, cosmetics, coiffure and body alternations as manifested in practices as varied as plastic surgery, tattooing, and ritual scarification. The series aims, in particular, to analyze the meaning of dress in relation to popular culture and gender issues and will included works grounded in anthropology, sociology, history, art history, literature, and folklore.

ISSN: 1360-466X

Previously published in the Series

Fashion-ology

An Introduction to Fashion Studies

Yuniya Kawamura

Oxford • New York

First published in 2005 by
Berg
Editorial offices:
First Floor, Angel Court, 81 St Clements Street, Oxford OX4 1AW, UK
175 Fifth Avenue, New York, NY 10010, USA

Paperback edition reprinted in 2005

Berg is the imprint of Oxford International Publishers Ltd.

Library of Congress Cataloging-in-Publication Data
Kawamura, Yuniya, 1963-
  Fashion-ology : an introduction to fashion studies / Yuniya Kawamura.
    p. cm
  Includes bibliographical references and index.
  ISBN 1-85973-809-5 (hardback : alk. paper) — ISBN 1-85973-814-1
(pbk. : alk., paper) 1. Fashion. 2. Fashion design. 3. Fashion
designers. 4. Clothing and dress — Symbolic aspects. I. Title

  TT519.K38 2005
  391 — dc22   2004023162

British Library Cataloguing-in-Publication Data
A catalogue record for this book is available from the British Library.

ISBN 1 85973 809 5 (hardback)
    1 85973 814 1 (paperback)

Typeset by Avocet Typeset, Chilton, Aylesbury, Bucks
Printed in the United Kingdom by Biddles Ltd, King's Lynn.

www.bergpublishers.com

To my family
Yoya, Yoko and Maya Kawamura

Contents

Contents

Acknowledgments

I am deeply grateful to Carol Poll, Chair of the Social Sciences Department at the Fashion Institute of Technology (F.I.T.)/State University of New York, for the constancy of her encouragement. I have benefited immensely from her support, wisdom and friendship.

My appreciation also goes to my other colleagues at F.I.T., Yasemin Celik, Toake Endoh, Jean-Ellen Giblin, Kevin MacDonald, Joseph Maiorca, Meg Miele, Ernest Poole, Roberta Paley, Laura Sidrowicz, Spencer Schein and Lou Zaera. Valerie Steele, Director of the Museum at F.I.T. has read some parts of this book which are taken from my doctoral dissertation, and she has given me informative comments.

Portions of the book were presented at several academic conferences: An International Conference on Fashion, Dress and Consumption in Brisbane, Australia, in July 2003; The Eastern Sociological Society in New York, in February, 2004; Costume Society of America in Houston, Texas, in May 2004, and IFHE (International Federation of Home Economics) in Kyoto, Japan, in August, 2004. I thank Reginetta Haboucha, Dean of the School of Liberal Arts, and the Teaching Institute at F.I.T. for funding parts of the travel.

I also thank Joanne Eicher, Editor of the *Dress, Body, Culture* Series, who gave me constructive comments and suggested that I split my original manuscript into two separate publications. I am also grateful to Kathryn Earle, Managing Director, and Ken Bruce, Production Manager, of Berg Publishers, along with all the editorial staff members. They constantly e-mailed me and updated me with every step of the publishing process.

I am also grateful to all my former colleagues and friends at the Nihon Kezai Shimbun in New York, Susumu Kurata, Norimichi Okai, Tsuneo Kita, Hiromichi Kaneko, Yuji Sonomoto, Hisao Saida and Ryo Abe, who have expressed their interest in my research.

Thanks also go to Yuri Sakashita-Fyfe, who sent me fashion-related articles all the way from New Zealand and took me to the Japanese fashion photography exhibition at the Powerhouse Museum in Sydney. Her friendship has been invaluable.

I also thank the patient and gracious assistance provided by the library staff at the Bibliothèque Forney, Bibliothèque Nationale de Paris, Columbia University, Institut Français de la Mode, Fashion Institute of Technology and Bunka School of Fashion.

I also appreciate a great deal of moral support Aki Kikuchi has given me, especially at the final stage of this project when I needed it most.

This book is dedicated to my family: my father, Yoya Kawamura who allowed me to continue my studies and to choose my own path in life; my mother, Yoko Kawamura who called me every week to check my well-being, and my sister, Maya Kawamura, who cooked for me whenever I was busy. I would not be who I am today without their love and support.

Yuniya Kawamura
New York

Introduction

Fashion-ology is a study of fashion. It is neither the study of dress nor the study of clothing, which means that the two, fashion and dress/clothing, are different concepts and entities which can be or should be studied separately. Fashion-ology is a sociological investigation of fashion, and it treats fashion as a system of institutions[1] that produces the concept as well as the phenomenon/practice of fashion. Similar to the sociology of art that studies the practices and institutions of artistic production (Wolff 1993: 139), Fashion-ology is also concerned with the social production process of the belief in fashion which exists in people's minds, and which begins to have a substance and life of its own. Items of clothing must go through the process of transformation to be labeled as fashion.

There has been a general tendency to ignore and neglect institutional factors in the discussions of fashion production. The primary focus of this book is the social nature of fashion in its production, distribution, diffusion, reception, adoption and consumption so that we can differentiate fashion production and fashion consumption from clothing production and clothing consumption. Therefore, since the process itself is the object of the study, a fashion-ological perspective of fashion requires no visual materials to explain fashion because it is not about clothing. However, it is difficult to deny the connection between fashion, that is an immaterial object, and clothing, that is a material object, because, as Brenninkmeyer (1963: 6) notes, clothing and dress are the raw material from which fashion is formed. Fashion as a belief is manifested through clothing.

Fashion-ology debunks the myth that the creative designer is a genius. Fashion is not created by a single individual but by everyone involved in the production of fashion, and thus fashion is a collective activity. Furthermore, a form of dress or a way of using it is not fashion or 'in fashion' until it has been adopted and used by a large proportion of people in a society. A particular style of dress has to be widely diffused and then accepted for anything to be fashion. However, the object has to be labeled as fashion before it reaches the consumption stage. It has to be recognizable as fashion. People are wearing clothes, but they believe or wish to believe that it is fashion that they are wearing and that they are consuming fashion and not clothing. That belief is born out of the socially constructed idea of fashion which means a great deal more than mere clothing.

There are multiple opinions of fashion, and we will see in subsequent chapters that opinions concerning the exact definition of fashion differ immensely. Which idea of fashion is to be accepted? For many authors, fashion first begins with clothing. The word 'fashion' is mainly used to refer to clothing and styles of appearance. There are 'fashions' in other aspects of intellectual and social life, and fashion exists in various spheres of our lives. It is a word that can be used in many senses, and we encounter and use the term 'fashion' every day loosely and ambiguously, generally meaning clothing-fashion. In order to understand what fashion means in a more specific sense, it is essential that we understand the difference between fashion and clothing and also integrate two senses of fashion, that is fashion as a concept and clothing-fashion as a practice or phenomenon. Only by interpreting fashion as a concept in a broader sense, do we understand what clothing-fashion means in a sociological sense. Fashion is a concept that separates itself from other words which are often used as synonyms of fashion, such as clothing, garments and apparel. Those words refer to tangible objects while fashion is an intangible object. Trying to define a particular item of clothing as fashion is futile because fashion is not a material product but a symbolic product which has no content substance by/in itself.

This book is intended as an introduction to fashion studies for students in any social science discipline but especially those in sociology of the arts, culture, occupation and/or organizations. In addition, those who study fashion design and the business side of fashion, for instance merchandising and marketing, could also benefit from this book as it describes the institutional processes through which designers and other fashion-related occupational groups go through. Fashion-ology involves the study of individual and institutional social networks in the world of fashion, giving a clearer picture and an understanding of how designers become famous and how their reputations are maintained and reproduced so that they continue to be the key players in fashion production. Such knowledge and information would be useful and meaningful for anyone who wishes to go into the fashion industry, which works to sustain people's belief in fashion.

Before I elaborate the structure and components of a fashion system that contributes to creating fashion as a belief, I will first examine the etymological origin of the term 'fashion' and further discuss the concept and the phenomenon of fashion. Furthermore, proponents and opponents of fashion will be investigated since fashion as an intellectual topic has been perceived as, on the one hand, too trivial and not worth spending time on and, on the other, a legitimate topic of analysis. I will then review empirical studies and discourses of fashion, dress and clothing in social sciences such as psychology, anthropology and history to understand how other social scientists besides sociologists[2] have treated fashion as a research topic and to see how their approaches may differ from or overlap with Fashion-ology, in terms of their analyses and the object of their study.

Etymology of Fashion

The terms 'fashion' and 'clothing' tend to be used synonymously, but while fashion conveys a number of different social meanings, clothing is the generic raw materials of what a person wears. The term 'fashion' in English, or 'la mode' in French, stands out from the other words, such as clothes, garment, attire, garb, apparel and costume, which are often referred to in relation to fashion.

According to *The Barnhart Dictionary of Etymology* (1988), it was probably about 1300 that a sense of style, fashion, manner of dress was first recorded. The *Dictionnaire de la mode au XXe siècle*[3] (Remaury 1996) indicates more specifically that the French word for fashion, which meant the collective manner of dressing, first appeared in 1482. The word originally comes from the word *modus* which means manner in English or *manière* in French. As for the etymology of the English word 'fashion,' it comes originally from the Latin *facio* or *factio* which means making or doing (Barnard 1996; Brenninkmeyer 1963: 2). In Old French it became *fazon*; in Middle French *facon*; then *façon* and *façonner* in French led to the Middle English word 'fashion,' meaning to make or a particular make or shape. By 1489, fashion had the meaning of a current usage, or a conventional usage in dress or lifestyle especially as observed in upper circles of society. The predominant social notion of of fashion arose early in the sixteenth century via the sense 'a special manner of making clothes' (Brenninkmeyer 1963: 2).

The New Oxford English Dictionary on Historical Principles published in 1901 defines the word 'fashion' primarily as the action/process of making, manner, a prevailing custom, a current usage, conventional usage in dress and mode of life. As 'the fashion,' it is defined as the mode of dress, etiquette, furniture and style of speech adopted in society for the time being. As synonyms of the word 'fashion,' words such as mode, style, vogue, trend, look, taste, fad, rage and craze are mentioned although there are slight differences in their meanings. 'Style' is sometimes the equivalent of fashion but also denotes conformity to a prevalent standard while 'vogue' suggests the temporary popularity of a certain fashion. Therefore, it seems agreed that fashion is never stationary, never fixed and ever-changing.

Barnard's study (1996) on fashion and clothing is one of the few studies that brings the two terms side by side trying to differentiate one from the other. Barnard makes an attempt to distinguish clothing from fashion and observes respective definitions, functions and meanings, but often treats the two simultaneously. Fashion and dress are used interchangeably because fashion is associated primarily with dress. Brenninkmeyer (1963: 5) also defines the words mode, clothing, dress, costume, custom and style among others (1963): 'Mode' is a synonym of fashion; 'clothing' originates from 'cloth' meaning a piece of woven or felted material made of wool, hair or cotton, suitable for wrapping or wearing, and in 1823, 'clothing' meant the distinctive dress worn by members of any profession. 'Dress' comes from the Middle French 'dresser' to English 'dress' meaning to arrange, and in general, it means the principal outergarments worn by women or the visible part of clothing. 'Costume' means mode of personal attire or dress belonging to a nation, class or period. As fashion has many interrelated aspects with these concepts (Brenninkmeyer 1963), it becomes impossible to demystify fashion as long as the focus is on the material objects.

Fashion as a Concept and a Phenomenon

What exactly is fashion? It is difficult to give an exact definition of fashion because the word has had different connotations throughout history; the meaning and significance of the word have changed to suit the social customs and clothing habits of people in different social structures. When fashion is treated as an item of clothing that has added value in a material sense, it confuses the notion of fashion. Fashion does provide extra added values to clothing, but the additional elements exist only in people's imaginations and beliefs. Fashion is not visual clothing but is the invisible elements included in clothing. Brenninkmeyer (1963: 4) defined fashion as a prevailing usage of dress adopted in society for the time being. It is the result of the acceptance of certain cultural values, all of which are open to relatively rapid influences of change.

Fashion as a concept means something more than the terms discussed above because it signifies additional and alluring values attached to clothing, which are enticing to consumers of 'fashion.' Finkelstein (1996) accurately points out that consumers imagine they are acquiring these added values when they are purchasing 'fashionable' items. Similarly, Bell (1976[1947]) argues persuasively that fashion is the essential virtue in a garment without which its intrinsic values can hardly be perceived; fashion encompasses the value added to clothing. However, these writers do not determine what precisely these values are. For instance, Paris as a brand is definitely one of the values, but scholars neglect to provide evidence as to how that value was produced. In subsequent chapters, I will discuss the institutionalization process of fashion and the making of a fashion system and fashion culture using Paris, the epitome of fashion, as an empirical case study.

As the concept of fashion changed historically, so did the phenomenon of fashion. The concept would not exist if the phenomenon did not exist. Fashion in the fifteenth century is something quite different from fashion in the nineteenth and the twentieth centuries. In the fifteenth century, fashion was an indicator of class status, a court privilege, practically monopolised by the aristocracy while the commoners would hardly have dared to call themselves fashionable; in the nineteenth century, social life had changed greatly (Boucher 1967/1987; Perrot 1994; Roche 1994). No longer did the aristocracy alone lead fashion, but the wealthy who had the material means were slowly invading into their social place (Perrot 1994; Sombart 1967[1902]). In the twentieth century, fashion became increasingly democratic, and everyone, regardless of rank or status, had a right to look fashionable.

No matter which time period in history one is talking about, the definite essence of fashion is change. The fashion process explains the diversity and changes of styles. Polhemus (1994, 1996) emphasized the association of fashion with an ideology of social change, and a situation in which change is also possible and desirable. In some societies where the dominant ideology is antipathetic to social change and progress, fashion cannot exist. Why does fashion change? One simplistic common view today is that fashion is the result of a conspiracy on the part of makers of clothes to make us spend more money, and that it is designers, clothing manufacturers and businesspeople who impose new fashions in order to stimulate the market and increase their trade. This may be an economic explanation but not a sociological one. The building of fashion cultures does not depend on the amount of money that consumers spend on clothing. I argue that a fashion system supports stylistic changes in fashion. The system provides the means whereby fashion change continually takes place.

Another fundamental element of fashion is believed to be ambivalence (Davis 1992; Flugel 1930). According to Flugel (1930), people's attitudes to dress have always been ambivalent, and there is the principal confrontation between emphasis on adornment on the one hand, and modesty or respectability on the other. Indeed, dress attempts to balance two contradictory aims: it focuses our attractions and at the same time protects our modesty. Koenig (1973) talked about the ambiguousness of public opinion concerning fashion, the ambivalent attitude to dress, an ambivalence of attitude in the positive or negative valuation of 'consumption.' More recently, Davis (1992) has also explained the ambivalent nature of fashion.

Novelty is also included as a crucial part of fashion, and it is highly valued in fashion. Koenig refers to ardent fashion followers as 'neophilia' (1973: 77) stating that humankind receptiveness for anything new is, among many other aspects, in some way essential to fashion-oriented behavior (Koenig 1973: 76). Similarly, Barthes correlates fashion to newness as follows:

> Fashion doubtless belongs to all the phenomena of neomania which probably appeared in our civilization with the birth of capitalism: in an entirely institutional manner, the new is a purchased value. But in our society, what is new in Fashion seems to have a well-defined anthropological function, one which derives from its ambiguity: simultaneously unpredictable and systematic, regular and unknown. (1967: 300)

On the other hand, Laver (1969) popularized the theory of erogenous zone drawn from psychoanalysis, and he explained that fashion rests on a supposed need for novelty to shift the erogenous zone so that different parts of the female body are emphasized by the changes in style. This view does not describe what happens as a result of fashion changes, but for Laver, it becomes an explanation of the system of fashion itself, which is very different from my employment of the term.

As Koenig (1973: 76) indicated, although the contents of fashion are always a manifestation of their epoch, its structural form as a special kind of the controlled behavior incorporates certain constants which decide initially what fashion is. Change and novelty are two of the characteristics that fashion encompasses. Fashion-ology makes an attempt to explain how institutions encourage and control these changes in style on a regular basis which simultaneously creates novelty. Contents of fashion, that is clothing, are constantly changing, but fashion as a form always remains in fashion cities.

Proponents and Opponents of Fashion

The study of fashion is of recent origin. Before fashion became a legitimate research topic for scholars, including social scientists, it was the topic often taken up by philosophers and moralists in the first half of the nineteenth century, and moral criticism and the criticism of fashion always went hand in hand (Koenig 1973: 31). In the early stages, there were those who were vehemently against fashion while there were others who supported it. Dress had also been the despair of the political economists and the administrators. Fashion was the privilege of the upper class of society, and the rest of the population wore local costume which was practically static, changing so slowly that it was hardly noticeable. Fashions were condemned because of their extravagances, and when they were worn by the wrong people, proper distinctions of rank were obliterated (Bell 1976[1947]: 23).

However, interest in fashion as a topic was aroused as fashion changes were taking place more and more rapidly. These rapid changes occurred as nineteenth-century industrialization resulted in the development of means for producing new fashion quickly and inexpensively. The social structure of the Western world underwent a great change in the eighteenth and nineteenth centuries: the population increased, productivity soared, money economy developed due to the growing division of labor, technology improved, commerce expanded and social mobility became possible. Without these factors, widespread fashion among the population as a whole would not have been possible, and as the fashion phenomenon became more democratized, it changed people's views on fashion.

Fashion as a Subject of Intellectual Discussion

Among European philosophers, the French philosopher Jean-Jacques Rousseau (1712–1780) was an opponent of luxury. In *Discours sur les sciences et les arts* (1750) he elaborated on the theory that Art acted as a negative force on manners and thought. For him, fashion destroyed virtue and masked vice. He said that the dissolution of morals and the necessary consequence of luxury bring about the corruption of taste. He became an outspoken critic of high society and its arts and sciences to the extent that they contributed to a world of luxury and hypocrisy repulsive to him. He was an advocate of simple living. In 1831, the English writer Thomas Carlyle published *Sartor Resartus* and wrote about the philosophy of clothes. Especially in those days, clothes were not yet considered a subject of earnest study, and they belonged to the sphere of the frivolous and the feminine, not worthy of serious consideration, only spoken of in learned circles to be derided and condemned for their extravagance and a lack of morality.

On the other hand, the French writer Honoré de Balzac (1799–1850) personally experienced the importance of the smallest nuances of behavior and ornament – for instance, the way a cravat was tied, how shoes were polished, the type of cigar smoked or how a cane was held – and understood how they were regarded with utmost seriousness by bourgeois consumers. All these subtle details of style were interpreted as significant markers of social standing (Williams 1982: 52). Similarly, the French poet Charles Baudelaire (1821–67) explored intellectually the distinctions between art and fashion, contemporary women and their fashion displays and the 'dandy.' Baudelaire talked of the pleasures of seeing a beautiful woman in contemporary costume rather than the ideal nude. Another French poet Stéphane Mallarmé (1842–98) was also a supporter of fashion, and he became the editor of a fashion journal titled *La Dernière Mode* (*The Latest Fashion*) which included commentary on clothing, fashion and travel.

However, fashion and/or clothing as a research topic have never been popular in social science disciplines. Almost all writers of fashion mention the academic devaluation of fashion as a topic in their introductory chapter before they begin. I am not an exception. Niessen and Brydon remark:

> Fashion and clothing have for a long while remained scholarly unmentionables. The unwillingness of social analysts to recognize the power of how people – of how they themselves – clothe, decorate, inscribe, perform and otherwise gesture with their bodies and avoidances ... Only recently, as some of the conventional barriers of academe crumble, have fashion and clothing matters been more incisively pursued and more credibly received. (1998: ix-x)

Similarly, Lipovetsky also explains why fashion as a topic is looked down upon in the academic field:

> The question of fashion is not a fashionable one among intellectuals ... Fashion is celebrated in museums, but among serious intellectual preoccupations it has marginal status. It turns up everywhere on the street, in industry, and in the media, but it has virtually no place in the theoretical inquiries of our thinkers. Seen as an ontologically and socially inferior domain, it is unproblematic and undeserving of investigation; seen as a superficial issue, it discourages conceptual approaches. (1994: 3–4)

Even professional writers of fashion find it difficult to explain what exactly fashion is. The history of dress is often seen as an area impervious to reason and analysis (Ribeiro 1995: 3). Wilson points out the complexity of explaining fashion:

Writings on fashion, other than purely descriptive, have found it hard to pin down the elusive double bluffs, the infinite regress in the mirror of the meanings of fashion. Sometimes fashion is explained in terms of an often over-simplified social history; sometimes it is explained in psychological terms; sometimes in terms of the economy. Reliance on one theoretical slant can easily lead to simplistic explanations that leave us still unsatisfied. (1985: 10)

Niessen and Brydon explain the development of studies of dress and fashion as follows:

Earlier writings within a positivist tradition by social psychologists, clothing and art historians, folklorists and sociologists have been expanded upon as theoretical advances reveal interconnections between material culture and social forms. Social analyses uniformly condemned fashion. Feminists critiqued the sexual politics and gender oppression inhering in clothing which hobble and confine women. Marxists critiqued the fetishism of fashion and the ideology of conspicuous consumption. Psychologists treated fashion adherence as pathology. However, slowly in 50's and 60's diverse writers4 were able to give theoretical weight to those people who understand their own thoughts and actions in relation to body decoration. (1998: x–xi)

The Feminization of Fashion

A major reason why fashion as a social phenomenon has been treated as futile is because the phenomenon is linked with outward appearance and women. Fashion is conceived as irrational because it changes constantly, has no content, works as an external decoration, and carries no intellectual elements. Early theorists of fashion (Simmel 1957[1904]; Veblen 1957[1899]) related the concept of fashion to the social position of women. Women were increasingly constructed as a spectacle even as they remained culturally invisible. Some argued that fashion gave women a compensation for their lack of position in a class-based social structure (Simmel 1957[1904]; Veblen 1957[1899]). Wives and daughters increasingly became vehicles of vicarious display; the wealth and prestige of the bourgeois male was displayed in the elegance of his wife and daughters who took on the endlessly demanding idle-work of being 'ladies' (Veblen 1957[1899]).

Fashion was not always a gendered phenomenon, and both men and women clothed themselves with elaborate costumes until the eighteenth century. Costume historians argue that in elite circles prior to the nineteenth century gender distinctions in dress were not nearly as strongly marked as they have become since. Men and women of the aristocracy and of the upper bourgeoisie who emulated it favored abundant displays of lace, rich velvets, fine silks, wore highly ornamented footwear, coiffures, wigs, and hats of rococo embellishment, and lavishly used scented powders, rouges and other cosmetics (Davis 1992). A pink silk suit, gold and silver embroidery, and jewelry were regarded as perfectly masculine (Steele 1988). Dress was the signifier of class. The more elaborate the dress, the higher its wearer's apparent social status. In short, fashion was not only a woman's affair. Fashion became feminized in the nineteenth century (Hunt 1996), and the representation of gender difference in dress became stronger than that of social class.

Along with the feminization of fashion, modernity is also characterized by a very distinct change in masculine identity. At the end of the eighteenth century, the bourgeois male underwent what has been called 'the great masculine renunciation,' which Flugel describes as 'the most remarkable event in the whole history of dress' (1930: 111). Men gave up their right to all the brighter, gayer and more varied forms of ornamentation, leaving these entirely to the use of women. Elite men abandoned their claim to be beautiful and aimed at being only useful. In today's post-industrial societies, the meanings of items of masculine clothing differ in various contexts, such as business and leisure settings, since men are more closely identified with the occupational sphere than women. Crane (2000) argues that today there is an age-segmentation of the clothing behavior of men while women are categorized as one, and she continues to explain that in our contemporary age-graded culture, the postmodern construction of non-occupational identities through clothing appears most strongly among the young and among racial and sexual minorities, whose members view themselves as marginal or exceptional in relation to the dominant culture.[5] Although we see that designer fashion for men attempts to extend the boundaries of acceptable forms of sexual expression for men, there is a gender division between female fashion and male fashion. Female fashion constitutes novelty and change, two important characteristics of fashion; the male population dresses conservatively in the workplace although leisure clothing seems to be gradually replacing traditional business clothing as in the 'business casual' dress code in force in many firms. Traditional male clothing styles have remained static – a characteristic which has little space in the realm of fashion.

Therefore, whilst men tend to be defined by their occupation, women's social roles are often discussed within the framework of women's interests in fashion and their supposed obsession with beauty.

Female Opponents of Fashion

Feminist scholars and writers were very much against fashion or fashionable individuals. As early as the late eighteenth century, Mary Wollstonecraft believed that too great an interest in self-adornment implies a diminution of the intellect and a mind disposed to frivolity (Ribeiro 1995: 3) and wrote: 'The air of fashion is but a badge of slavery . . . which many young people are so eager to attain, always strikes me like the studied attitudes of some modern prints, copied with tasteless servility after the antique; the soul is left out, and none of the parts are tied together by what may properly be termed character' (Wollstonecraft 1792: 220).

Finkelstein explains how fashion is perceived from a feminist's point of view:

> Feminist readings of fashion have often portrayed it as a kind of conspiracy to distract women from the real affairs of society, namely economics and politics. Fashion has been seen as a device for confining women to an inferior social order, largely because it demands an unequal expenditure of time and money by women on activities which do not attract the professional attention and efforts of men. Fashion works to intensify self-absorption and thereby reduces the social, cultural and intellectual horizons of women. (1996: 56)

Thus, for contemporary feminists, the relationship between female liberation and female beauty, including women's concern about appearance, is crucial (Brownmiller 1984; Tseelon 1995). Personal appearance defines the woman's social position and also influences the way she comes to think of herself. The feminist debate about dress and attitudes to personal adornment indicates that fashionable dress tends to be construed as part of the oppression of women. To care about dress and physical appearance is oppressive and women's love of clothes is a form of 'false consciousness'[6] (Tseelon 1995). The dominant feminist perspective on fashion or beauty is that fashion emerges out of the desire to be beautiful, the norm for which is created by men in a male-dominated society.

Devotion to fashion in dress was adduced as a natural weakness of women, something they could not help. This view was strengthened in the nineteenth century when masculine and feminine clothing became so much more different in fabric, trim and construction. Elegant men's clothing during this time was actually no less complex, demanding, and uncomfortable, but it tended to be more subdued and abstract in the way it looked. Women's clothing was extremely expressive and very deliberately decorative and noticeable (Hollander 1980: 360). Therefore, as Wilson indicates:

Fashion has been a source of concern to feminists, both today and in an earlier period. Feminist theory is the theorization of gender, and in almost all known societies the gender division assigns to women a subordinate position. Within feminism, fashionable dress and the beautification of the self are conventionally perceived as expressions of subordination; fashion and cosmetics fixing women visibly in their oppression. (1985: 13)

Craik (1994: 44) points out that Western fashion became preoccupied with techniques of femininity the women strived to achieve feminine qualities and traits from the eighteenth century, and she refers to techniques of dress and decoration as fashion systems that manifest techniques of gender that are specific to any cultural formation. This phenomenon is probably almost universal and not confined to the Western world.

Female Proponents of Fashion

In contrast to the views above, one can look at the link between women and fashion positively in the postmodern interpretation where the breakdown of identity is found, and fashion plays no role in the oppression of women. As Wilson persuasively explains:

in 'denaturalizing the wearer's spectacular identity' contemporary fashion refuses the dichotomy nature/culture. Fashion in our epoch denaturalizes the body and thus divests itself of all essentialism. This must be good news for women since essentialism ideologies have been oppressive to them. Fashion often plays with, and playfully transgresses gender boundaries, inverting stereotypes and making us aware of the masque of femininity. (1994: 187)

Using fashion as a tool, women shift from nature to culture. Focusing on beauty and fashion is feminist in so far as it is a source of power and controlled by women themselves. It is male control over it giving women no autonomy that becomes problematic. The conflict between fashion and feminism is an unresolved, ongoing issue that requires further in-depth research.

Moreover, we need to detach our views from a gendered perspective of fashion because it is limited in understanding fashion as a sociological concept. It is necessary to bring fashion to a much larger spectrum of a social system and ask why it exists in that particular system. The feminization of fashion was tied to the decline of European aristocracy and the corresponding ascendancy of the bourgeoisie, a movement that, though much accelerated by the French Revolution, was well underway before 1789 (Hunt 1996). Protestant-oriented values of hard work, sobriety, frugality, and personal economic advancement figured prominently in the structural transformation of European society (Weber 1947). Perhaps it was essentially the desire of the bourgeoisie to reflect these moral attitudes in what they wore that accounted for men and women coming to dress so distinctively (Davis 1992). Therefore, in order to analyze fashion or clothing-fashion as a sociological topic, we must place it in a social context along with social change. Lipovetsky (1994) postulates that the study of fashion needs new impctus, renewed questioning because fashion is a trifling, fleeting, 'contradictory' object par excellence. For that very reason it ought to provide a good stimulus for theoretical argument. Fashion may be socially frivolous but it is not sociologically trivial. Fashion is the result of a great deal of influence which collectively determines the social structure of society.

Before discussing sociological studies of fashion in the next chapter, let us first examine different studies of fashion in other areas of social science, such as Psychology, Social Psychology, History, Art History, Cultural Anthropology and Economics.

Studies of Fashion in Social Science

Before elaborating on the concept of fashion as a system, I investigate studies of fashion in the social science discipline and research methods they have utilized to analyze fashion and/or clothing. Fashion, however conceived, is extremely difficult to measure and research unless the units of analysis are accurately determined.

According to Roach-Higgins and Eicher (1973: 26–7), social scientists have begun to take interest in dress and fashion only recently. In the late 1920s and the 1930s came an upsurge of interest in publications on the psychological, social and cultural implication of dress, and this interest no doubt was associated with general sharp breaks with tradition at that time, symbolized so well in the dress of women[7] (Roach-Higgins and Eicher 1973: 29–30).

Fashion gradually became a concern for sociologists and psychologists who were interested in studying the motives stimulating individual and group behavior, including clothing behavior. As early as 1876, Herbert Spencer, a sociologist, examined the role played by fashion in the society of his time. He lived in a changing social structure and saw fashion as a part of social evolution. In 1904, Simmel, an expert in seeing the dualistic side of social phenomena, saw fashion as the desire for imitation and differentiation, and many other sociologists and social scientists (Sumner

1940[1906]; Tarde 1903; Toennies 1963[1887]; Veblen 1957[1899]) shared his view. Sociological discourse and empirical studies of fashion will be discussed fully in the next chapter.

While sociologists sought the motives governing fashion in group behavior, authors with a psychological approach, on the other hand, often based their argument on one instinct as responsible for fashion phenomenon. Psychologists are concerned with the basic concepts of motivation, learning and perception, and they argue much clothing behavior is psychological in nature. By using psychology as a framework for study, clothing can be seen as an intimate part of the personality or self (Horn and Gurel 1975: 2). Hurlock explains how close clothes can be to our bodies: 'We are apt to think of clothes as we do of our bodies, and so to appropriate them that they become perhaps more than any of our other possessions, a part of ourselves ... in spite of the constant changes in clothing, it is still impossible to disassociate ourselves from this intimate part of our material possessions' (1929: 44).

If psychology is the study of individual behavior and sociology is the study of group behavior, subject matter that falls within the overlapping areas between these two disciplines constitutes a third field of study, social psychology. Ross (1908) in his study discussed the contagions of collective behavior that result in group action. Ryan (1966) attempted to coordinate findings based on many different theoretical premises and classed them according to their general social psychological significance. Horn and Gurel explain:

> on the basis of social psychological research, as well as on the points of agreement found in some early writings concerning the interpretation of clothing behavior, we see that clothing is a symbol of crucial importance to the individual. As a non-verbal language, it communicates to others an impression of social status, occupation, role, self-confidence, intelligence, conformity, individuality, and other personality characteristics. (1975: 2)

Barnard takes a similar approach to fashion and clothing as communication:

> the things people wear are significant or meaningful, and it has attempted to explain what sort of meanings fashion and clothing may have, how those meanings are produced or generated, and how fashion and clothing communicate those meanings ... meaning, like fashions, were not static or fixed ... .even the use of the term 'fashion' was not static or fixed, that it was a product of the context in which it appeared and that an item could function as fashion at one moment as clothing, or anti-fashion, at another. (1996: 171)

On the other hand, Langner (1959) referred to Adler's refinements on psychoanalytic theory, notably the concepts of inferiority and superiority as explanatory of dress.

Traditionally, the study of fashion and/or clothing has been a brand of art history and has followed its methods of attention to detail. Comparable to the study of furniture, painting and ceramics, a major part of its project has been accurate dating of costume, assignment in some cases of 'authorship,' and an understanding of the actual process of the making of the garment, all of which are valid activities (Wilson 1985: 48). Historians and art historians (Boucher 1987[1967]; Davenport 1952; Hollander 1993, 1994; Steele 1985, 1988, 1991) look at clothing and dress over extended periods, and they explain repeated regularities and fluctuation and decode the cultural meanings of dress and clothing. This is a very difficult task since there is little data beyond 150 years; there is not exact knowledge before the year 1800 (Roach-Higgins and Eicher 1973). From then, we can find abundant information due to the early fashion magazines, fashion plates and the fashion dolls which were sent primarily from Paris to different parts of the world.

Cultural anthropologists make cross-cultural comparisons of traditional, non-industrialized societies in terms of dress. Their studies help us understand that using clothing to express modesty is a function that is determined by the culture, learned by the individuals and is not instinctive in nature. People cover or decorate their bodies for a variety of reasons and modesty is one of them. Other reasons include protection, the desire to be sexually attractive and adornment.

Some scholars, such as Sombart (1967[1902]), Nystrom (1926) and Anspach (1967), approach fashion from an economic point of view. Sombart saw the connection between fashion and economics and remarked: 'Fashion is capitalisim's favourite child' (1967[1902]). He denied any part that the consumer plays in creating fashion and has to accept what the producer offers, and he stressed that it is the producer that shapes fashion while the consumer accpets what is offered to him/her. Nystrom (1928) examined the cause of fashion, the fashion cycle, trends in fashion and fashion prediction while Anspach (1967) emphasized clothing as a commodity.

We can see that the unit of analysis in almost all studies of fashion is clothes and dress, and no scholars clearly distinguish fashion from clothing or vice versa. This is what Fashion-ology attempts to do.

The Use of Visual Materials as Evidence

Different types of visual records have been used to research dress and fashion. Writers of fashion, especially art historians, who examine fashion from the wearer's point of view, look specifically at the actual garments. As part of visual culture, fashion is frequently being studied through illustrations, paintings and photographs. Fashion historians (Steele 1985; Hollander 1993) use historical materials, such as periodicals, store catalogues, advertisements, pamphlets and paintings among others, as evidence to investigate how people dressed and what people wore hundreds and thousands years ago.

Roach-Higgins and Eicher explain how dress has been recorded in many different forms in the past:

> sculpture, paintings and ceramics ... provided visual representations from very ancient times. Pictorial textiles and printed plates showing dress, as well as actual costume artifacts, are available from about the sixteenth century ... Costume histories summarize data from many of these sources. Modern costume histories are made more exact through the use of photographs of actual objects, often in color ... While contemporary items of dress are readily available, artifacts are limited, and many are destroyed and have deteriorated. Costume plates and fashion plates were also used. (1973: 11–17)

For visual information from before the second half of the nineteenth century the works of painters, including the earliest cavepeople who practiced their art on the walls of their caves as well as their numerous descendants who have recorded their impressions of human appearance on various surfaces, and those of sculptors who have modeled recognizable human forms from clay, wood, ivory and rough chunks of stone, have been used (Roach-Higgins and Eicher 1973: 6–8; Taylor 2002).

Although it is difficult to rely solely on written documents, they could also be used as a supplementary material in the studies of fashion and dress. Since artists may deviate from exact, visual representations, the accuracy of their pictures needs to be determined by other available data. One way to check is to refer to written descriptions and commentaries on dress of the same period in history, such as personal diaries, accounts of travel and exploration, catalogues, biographies, novels, memoirs, essays, satires, books of history and philosophy and manuals on etiquette and personal conduct (Taylor 2002); religious writings can also be rich sources of information on dress although they may be written for other purposes and have nothing to do with fashion per se. These written forms of evidence can provide information to help validate the authenticity of visual representations and to elucidate the meaning of dress within its contemporary setting, although they, too, may be subject to bias (Roach-Higgins and Eicher 1973: 15).

Quantitative Methods

In opposition to qualitative methods discussed above, some scholars have made an attempt to measure garments that appeared in various magazines although this is not a common way to study clothing and fashion. One of the earliest quantitative studies of fashion was conducted by an American anthropologist, Kroeber (1919). He studied the fashion process and cycles by presenting a series of measurements of fashion changes over a specific time period and took measurements from fashion magazines and journals between 1844–1919. He took eight measurements, four of which were the lengths and four of which were the widths of a dress. He focused on women's formal silk evening dresses because these have served the same definite occasions for more than a century, according to Kroeber. The absolute numbers were converted into percentage ratios to the length of the entire figure as it has been defined. Then the percentage for each measure was averaged for each year. Kroeber came to the conclusion that the details of fashion change more often than the general fashion trend.

Similarly, Young (1966[1939]) obtained data from fashion magazines and made a quantitative analysis. Her central argument is that fashion change is essentially cyclical and is independent of historical events, epochs of thought, ideals or artistic periods. She gives a continuous annual series of illustrations of the most 'typical' costumes worn from 1760 through 1937. In order to select the typical fashion of a particular year, she chooses from fashion magazines of that year fifty illustrations of daytime, street dresses. These are then sorted over and tabulated to determine the type of skirt that appeared the largest number of times. The process is then repeated to select the most favored type of collar, of sleeve, of waist, and of belt. The result is a number of 'typical' components, each representing a different part of the costume of that year. A single illustration combining all of them is considered an 'annual typical.' However, this definition of 'annual typical' and who determined the typical styles of the season must be questioned. Treating one particular style as the standard style of a specific time frame is not possible, especially in contemporary postmodern society where the source of fashion is being decentralized (Crane 2000). Kroeber (1919) and Young (1966[1939]) took the measurements of garments to investigate regularities in social change, but I question the accuracy and significance of taking these measurements which are varied and subtle. If researchers need to pay attention to the intrinsic nature, quality and measurements of clothes and wish to work with real garments, I urge them to examine the technical production process as I did in a recent study (Kawamura 2004). Quantitative methods require analytic scrutiny, exact measuring, careful recording and judgment on the basis of observed fact, and this is difficult to attain when the unit of analysis is the garment itself.

Outline of the Book

Chapter 1 has been a introductory chapter outlining the main theme of the book and explaining why fashion and clothing can be studied separately. Studies of fashion in social sciences and research methodologies have been discussed. It has also explained why fashion as an intellectual topic is often considered trivial and frivolous while there are strong proponents of fashion. Chapter 2 examines classical and contemporary sociological discourse as well as empirical studies of fashion and places fashion within the study of sociology of culture by treating fashion as a manufactured cultural symbol. Chapters 1 and 2 lay the foundation for the future discussion of Fashion-ology. The theoretical underpinnings of Fashion-ology are found in Chapter 3, and a distinct approach to fashion as an institutionalized system is elaborated while I examine various studies of fashion systems to show how my employment of the term 'a fashion system' overlaps with and/or differs from others. An empirical study of the fashion system in Paris will be briefly explained. Chapters 4 and 5 include the discussions of individuals and institutions in the fashion system who help maintain the ideology of fashion that is supported by the system. Designers, who are the major players in the system, personify the concept of fashion while journalists, editors and advertisers contribute to the production, gatekeeping and dissemination of fashion. Chapter 6 examines the role that consumers play in fashion adoption and the way they use fashion as a symbolic strategy, and it also explains how consumers today are becoming producers, and thus the boundary between consumption and production of fashion is disappearing. Chapter 7 is the conclusion of the book.

2

Sociological Discourse and Empirical Studies of Fashion

This chapter investigates how earlier and contemporary sociologists discuss fashion within a larger theoretical framework of culture and society. I identify the reasons and the need for sociologists to conduct research on fashion despite its academic devaluation explained in the previous chapter. The review of classical and contemporary discourse and empirical studies on fashion provides readers the bases for understanding and acknowledging fashion as a significant scholarly and sociological theme. These discussions, in addition to the literature about the arts and artists (Becker 1982; Bourdieu 1984; White and White 1965[1993]; Wolff 1983, 1993; Zolberg 1990), serve as the foundation for Fashion-ology. I will also place fashion within the study of sociology of culture and treat fashion as a manufactured cultural symbol.

The classical discourse of fashion is categorized according to the writers' theoretical approaches which involve overlapping concerns though the emphases differ. While they all relate fashion to the concept of imitation, some treat it as a sign of democratic society and others use it as an expression of class distinction. Although none of the classical writers use the term 'trickle-down theory,' their basic premise is that the fashions are supposed to trickle down from the higher classes to the lower classes. Many contemporary writers oppose the view, and they argue that fashion is not a product of class differentiation and emulation but a response to a wish to be up to date and to express new tastes which are emerging in a changing world (Blumer 1969a).

Fashion implies a certain fluidity of the social structure of the community, and it requires a particular type of society, that is the modern world where the social stratification system is open and flexible. There must be differences of social position, but it must seem possible and desirable to bridge these differences. Therefore, fashion is not possible in a rigid hierarchy.

Classical Sociological Discourse of Fashion

Classical sociologists at the turn of the twentieth century (Simmel 1957[1904]; Spencer 1966[1896]; Sumner 1940[1906], Summer and Keller 1927; Tarde 1903; Toennies 1963[1887]; Veblen 1957[1899]) theorize and conceptualize the notion of fashion, and they show us the sociological importance and perspective of fashion.

Fashion as Imitation

What earlier sociologists share in the discussion of fashion is the concept of imitation. It is a relational concept which is necessarily a social relationship and, therefore, of sociological significance. These sociologists explain how fashion, which is a process of imitation, is included in understanding culture and society. Imitation, which is at the basis in making an analysis of fashion, is typically a view from above since it assumes that social inferiors envy superiors and engage in imitative activities to emulate their 'betters' in order to gain recognition and even entry into the privileged group (Hunt 1996). For Spencer, fashion is intrinsically imitative: 'Imitative, then, from the beginning, first of a superior's defects, and then, little by little, of other traits peculiar to him, fashion has ever tended towards equalization. Serving to obscure, and eventually to obliterate, the marks of class distinction, it has favored the growth of individuality' (1966[1897]: 205–6). He posits two types of imitations: reverential and competitive. Reverential imitation is prompted by reverence for the one imitated. For instance, any modification of dress adopted by a king is imitated by courtiers and spreads downwards; the result of this process is 'fashion' in clothing. This is a fundamental principle of a 'trickle-down' theory of fashion. Competitive imitation is prompted by the desire to assert equality with a person.

Veblen's discussion of fashion (1957[1899]) remains within the framework of the creation and institutionalization of the leisure class through consumption activities. He identifies three properties of fashion: 1) It is an expression of the wearer's wealth. Expenditure on clothing is a striking example of conspicuous consumption. Clothes are the evidence and indication of economic wealth at the first glance. What is not expensive is unworthy and inferior. 2) It shows that one does not need to earn one's living or is not engaged in any kind of productive physical labor. Elaborately elegant, neat, spotless garments imply leisure. The less practical and functional a garment is, the more it is a symbol of high class. Some styles always require a help to wear them. 3) It is up to date. It must be 'in fashion' which means that it must be appropriate for the present time. While the second point is not applicable to today's fashion phenomenon because practicality or impracticality of a style does not define what is fashion, the first and third points must be considered in depth. In subsequent chapters, I will explain which types of clothing serve the purpose of conspicuous consumption and how fashion as an institutionalized system makes and determines what is fashionable.

No writer places more emphasis on imitation than Tarde (1903); imitation is the key to his overall social theory. Tarde elaborates his thought largely through three central concepts: invention, imitation and opposition. Inventions, the creations of talented individuals, are disseminated throughout social systems by the process of imitation. These imitations spread, regularly progressing toward the limits of the system until they come into contact with some obstacle. The three processes form an interdependent relationship, continuing to generate and influence one another in multiple ways. Upper-class women invent new styles, and when they are imitated, in order to express their oppositions, these women come up with newer styles. Like Spencer (1996[1886]), Tarde (1903) postulates that social relations are essentially imitative relationships. Thus, fashion with its imitative nature is a crucial phenomenon in understanding society. He holds, like many others, that fashion fundamentally consists of the imitation of a few superiors by a great number of inferiors.

Fashion as Class Distinction: Inclusion and Exclusion

In contrast to other classical sociologists (Simmel 1957[1904]; Spencer 1966[1896]; Sumner 1940[1906], Sumner and Keller 1927; Tarde 1903; Toennies 1963[1887]) who argue that imitation is a positive behavior, Veblen 1957[1899]) degrades the act of imitation since the imitation remains merely an imitation, that is a second-order, second-rate reproduction. Nothing can compensate for the lack of 'real' products such as 'real' pearls or 'real' silk; in other words, the materials employed must be difficult to obtain or laborious to produce. Veblen explains:

> We all find a costly hand-wrought article of apparel much preferable, in point of beauty and of serviceability, to a less expensive imitation of it, however cleverly the spurious article may imitate the costly original; and what offends our sensibilities in the spurious article is not that it falls short in form or color, or, indeed, in visual effect in any way. The offensive object may be so close an imitation as to defy any but the closest scrutiny; and yet so soon as the counterfeit is detected, its aesthetic value, and its commercial value as well, declines precipitately. (1957[1899]: 81)

Veblen argues that increasing wealth made the ruling class pay attention to the display of leisure as well as leisure goods. This 'conspicuous consumption' is at once an expression of wealth and a demonstration of purchasing power. In his theory, he discusses why some consumers prefer to pay more but does not indicate how they come to know which objects would fulfill the purposes of conspicuous consumption or how the value of an object is created and determined.

In Spencer's view, fashion is a symbol of manifestation of relationships between superiors and inferiors that functions as a social control. Various forms of obeisance through mutilations, presents, visits, forms of address, titles, badges, and costumes express domination and submission, and thus, fashion is a symbol of social rank and status (Spencer 1966[1896]). Although Spencer does not make an explicit distinction between clothing and fashion, he implies that what is important is not the actual clothes that are worn, but the wearer's position in society, which has the power to transform clothing into fashion.

Like Spencer, Toennies (1961[1909]) argues that we follow fashion 'slavishly' to indicate our acceptance of the leadership of those who dominate the groups in which we desire membership, just as we follow the customs and traditions of such groups as an indication of our desire to remain among or join them. This interpretation is similar to Simmel's (1957[1904]) argument. Simmel points out that, in addition to imitation, demarcation constitutes an important factor in fashion since the act of imitation arises out of the desire for class distinction. He argues that fashion serves to unite a given class and to segregate it from other classes. It poses a threat to the upper bourgeois class and offers an opportunity to the lower working class to cross that class boundary. Simmel postulates (1947[1904]: 546): 'the fashions for the upper classes develop their power of exclusion against the lower in proportion as general culture advances, at least until the mingling of the classes and the leveling effect of democracy exert a counter-influence.'

Therefore, for Simmel, fashion is a form of both imitation and social equalization, but paradoxically, in changing incessantly, it differentiates one time from another and one social stratum from another. It unites those of a social class and segregates them from others. The elite initiates a fashion and, when the mass imitates it in an effort to obliterate the external distinctions of class, abandons it for a newer mode; this is a process that speeds up with the increase of wealth. Fashion contains the attraction of highly changeable differentiation. Likewise, if one is dressed in such a way that one cannot engage in menial physical labor, one is marked as a member or dependent of the leisure class, or at least as someone who for a time can 'dress the part' of a member of that class (Veblen 1957[1899]).

Fashion as Social Custom

Sumner (1940[1906]), see also Sumner and Keller 1927) and Toennies (1963[1887]) treat fashion as a social custom. Sumner locates the notion of fashion in a much larger perspective, including fashion in clothing. He regards a large array of human activities, beliefs and artifacts as fashions. His definition of fashion includes usages like kissing, shaking hands, bowing, and smiling in conversation, which, according to Sumner, are all controlled primarily by fashion. He argues that fashion is an aspect of mores, and it may affect any form of human activity. Sumner also discusses fashion and clothing in connection with imitation. Summer and Keller explain:

> Those who follow it are practicing a sort of imitation sometimes enthusiastic, but oftener simply enforced by fear. It extends all the way from dress and ornament to ideals of character and favorite objects of enthusiasm and devotion ... Then come social contagion and imitation; the crowd falls into line and follows the path which has been lightly worn by a sparse vanguard. (1927: 324)

The term 'folkways' was coined by Sumner to describe norms that are simply the customary, normal, habitual ways a group does things. Folkways is a broad concept that covers relatively permanent traditions, and he gives examples such as the Christmas tree, the white wedding dress, as well as short-lived fads and fashions. A key feature of all folkways is that there is no strong feeling of right or wrong attached to them. They are simply the way people usually do things.

Similarly, Toennies is influenced by Spencer's account of fashion and relates it to custom. His *Community and Society* (1963[1887]) contrasts a personalistic traditional type of society with the impersonal, rational, modern society. His polar types of society are based on two kinds of human interaction. Toennies describes custom as a kind of 'social will' formed through habit and from practices based on tradition. Custom points toward the past and we legitimize it through traditional usage. Custom determines not only ancient cult practices but also the manner and form of rites and ceremonies.

This power of custom seems to wane and die in times of revolution and great social change, such as a time of transition from community (*Gemeinschaft*) to society (*Gesellschaft*). Customs are unwritten laws. The essence of custom is practice, what we actually do in our social relations, and it also signifies community. What begins as a mark of distinction often ends as common custom. Toennies, despite not using Spencer's term, suggests that, when reverential imitation occurs, the manners of people of distinction are copied by their inferiors as well as subordinates and new manners must be created by those who wish to distinguish themselves from their imitators. The manners of the elites are distinct from those of the lower ranks in society. Elites base their manners in common custom, but at the same time do everything possible to differentiate their manners from the customs of the common people.

Toennies discusses custom in clothing, which fixes and orders what would otherwise be arbitrary. It establishes certain dress as feminine and masculine, as well as other differences in social role such as unmarried and widowed, youth and adult, or master and servant. Clothing is used to legitimize the wearer's position in symbolic identifications with traditions already powerful in their society. Outward appearances are all we really can achieve. Clothing among country people is a genuine expression of custom when it is worn as regional or national dress. Urban elite dress differs from such costume in its function as symbol of class or rank. Some forms of urban dress remain subject to custom because preferences in such dress remain subject to social beliefs and traditions. Distinction in dress is very different where fashion dominates. Desire for distinction is expressed in frequent change of dress, and in frequent discard of what has already been worn. The drive for distinction weakens the power of tradition and this is the beginning of fashion as well as *Gesellschaft*.

Fashion, Modernity and Social Mobility

By understanding imitation as a characteristic of fashion among many others, we learn that it requires a certain kind of social system for imitation to occur or for imitation to be 'allowed' to occur. Imitation is something that must be permitted by authority, which in turn implies the thrust toward equality that characterizes a modern democratic social system (Spencer 1966[1896]). In medieval and early modern Europe, sumptuary laws prohibited people in the subordinate ranks from living or dressing like those above them. However, as industrialism in a less hierarchical society made wealth and ranks more flexible, people became wealthy enough to compete in style of living with those above them in rank.

This development signifies that fashion both requires a certain degree of mobility and fluidity within a society and promotes a more egalitarian society and erases class boundaries. Fashion phenomena occur only in a particular social context that allows social mobility. Immobility in the distribution of vestimentary signs always corresponds to immobility in social structures (Perrot 1994). Prior to the sixteenth century, there was minimal mobility in Europe where social roles and statuses were rigidly fixed, often by law and certainly by custom. Thus fashion did not emerge in society. According to Tarde, Spencer, Simmel and Toennies, fashion functions as an equalizing mechanism because imitation is one of the means to reducing the inequality, suppressing caste, class and national barriers. The lower strata gradually rise, step by step to the highest ranks. Through assimilation and imitation, inequality is no longer aristocratic but democratic inequality (Tarde 1903). Thus social superiority is no longer hereditary but individual.

Therefore, the origins of fashion lie in the origins of modernity with the growth of industrial capitalism. Koenig's discussion of modernity and the link between the emergence of fashion and democratization is compelling.

> Certainly, the radical difference between the old upper class and the lower classes has disappeared. But this does not mean that the minor differences need also disappear. On the contrary ... minor differences can be felt far more strongly when general equality has won the day. It could be said that in the modern mass civilization of the advanced industrial societies it is not the great contrasts, but the delicate differences that are effective; the delicate difference is the most perfect expression of the increasing democratization of society. This applies not only to politics but also to fashion consumption. (1973: 65)

Thus fashion plays a significant role in the manifestation of subtle differences. The class boundary has become blurry, and people wish to make subtle distinctions in order to differentiate themselves from others. This is what fashion in the modern world has become. Because there are more opportunities for everyone, the competition is more democratic and the right to participate in the competition is prevalent; at the same time, fashion as a concept and clothing-fashion as a phenomenon and practice emerge in many societies. As Simmel points out:

> People like fashion from outside and such foreign fashions assume greater values within the circle, simply because they did not originate there. The exotic origin of fashions seems strongly to favor the exclusiveness of the groups which adopt them ... This motive for foreignness which fashion employs in its socializing endeavors, is restricted to higher civilization. (1957[1904]: 545–6)

The newness which, as noted earlier, is the essence of fashion is the typical condition of modernity and postmodernity. The desire for change is characteristic of cultural life in industrial capitalism, which fashion expresses so well (Wilson 1985), but at the same time postmodern society is a society driven to create, not only novelty, but a perpetual desire for need and for endless difference (Barnard 1996). Whether analyzing modernity or postmodernity, one thing that analysts all tend to agree on is that it is fashion, and not dress or clothing, that is the topic under consideration. The same characteristics of fashion are being used to exemplify both modernity and postmodernity. Furthermore, modern and postmodern societies are both societies in which mobility is possible and desirable, and as Baudrillard (1981, 1993[1976]) explains, fashion appears only in socially mobile societies, although not all the mobile, open-class societies have fashion. Baudrillard emphasizes fashion as a modern phenomenon: 'Fashion only exists in the framework of modernity . . . In politics, in technology, in art, in culture, modernity defines itself by the rate of change tolerated by the system without really changing anything in the essential order . . . Modernity is a code and fashion is its emblem.' Furthermore, he states:

> The formal logic of fashion imposes an increased mobility on all the distinctive social signs. Does this formal mobility of signs correspond to a real mobility in social structures (professional, political, cultural)? Certainly not. Fashion – and more broadly, consumption, which is inseparable from fashion – masks a profound social inertia. It itself is a factor of social inertia, insofar as the demand for real social mobility frolics and loses itself in fashion, in the sudden and often cyclical changes of objects, clothes and ideas. And to the illusion of change is added the illusion of democracy. (1981: 78)

For Baudrillard, fashion is one of those institutions that best restores cultural inequality and social discrimination, establishing them under the pretense of abolishing them. Fashion is governed by the social strategy of class.

The Origin of Fashion Phenomenon

While Finkelstein (1996: 23) remarks that fashion is a versatile social and psychological mechanism that lacks a fixed point of origin, Lipovetsky and many others argue that fashion as a concept emerged as the phenomenon of fashion began. While clothes are almost universal, fashion is not. Fashion does not belong to all ages or to all civilizations; it has an identifiable starting point in history (Lipovetsky 1994). Fashion is an outstanding mark of modern civilization (Blumer 1969a). J.C. Flugel (1930) specifically indicates that fashion is linked to a particular society and culture, those of the West. Bell (1976[1947]: 105) also points out that fashion, as we know it in the West, is not and never was a universal condition of dress. It is a European product and is not nearly as old as European civilization, and it is an expanding force, it affects an ever greater number of people in an ever greater part of the world although the expansion of fashion has not been a regular phenomenon.

On the other hand, Craik (1994) questions whether fashion can be confined to the development of European fashion and argues that the term 'fashion' needs revision because fashion is too often equated with modern European high fashion. Similarly, Cannon (1998: 24) says that because fashion is normally seen as a more recent and specifically Western development, its role in the creation of style among smaller-scale societies is generally unrecognized. Cannon (1998: 23) argues that current definition of fashion excludes the systematic changes in style that occur in all cultures, and that in smaller-scale societies systematic style change may only occur sporadically as it is activated by circumstances, and continue only so long as the conducive conditions exist. Therefore, a more inclusive definition of fashion must encompass the basic process of style change, without the requirement that it be the continuous process evident in recent Western industrial societies (Cannon 1998: 23).

Are there societies without fashion? If so, in what social context does fashion exist? Is the system of changing styles of dress universal? Whether fashion is universal or not, or whether fashion is a Western phenomenon or not, all depends on how one defines fashion. Indeed, fashion can be applied to non-industrialized, non-Western cultures depending on the definition of fashion. Like Craik (1994), Cannon strongly disagrees with the perspective that fashion is a Western phenomenon and argues: 'Although the processes of fashion comparison, emulation and differentiation are more noticeably apparent in the rapid changes that characterize systems of industrial production, the same processes are observable or at least inferable in most cultures . . . The universality of fashion is . . . evident in its general definition as an agent of style change' (1998: 23). Based on her premise, therefore, fashion is found not only in modern societies but exists in all known societies.

Explanations of fashion, as defined in recent Western contexts, typically focus on its psychological motivation and social purpose (Blumer 1969a; Sproles 1985). Its psychologcial basis, which is the desire to create a positive self-image, is recognized as widely if not universally applicable cross-culturally, but the social role of fashion is often restricted by definition to those societies that exhibit a clearly-defined class structure (McKendrick, Brewer and Plumb 1982; Simmel 1957[1904]). This definition is unnecessarily restrictive, and ignores pervasive but much more subtle distinctions in status based on personality, wealth and skill. These are equally capable of giving rise to fashion-based differentiation and emulation, especially in circumstances where the basis for prestige recognition is uncertain or undergoing change (Cannon 1998: 24). Cannon continues:

> fashion is an inherent part of human social interaction and not the creation of an elite group of designers, producers, or marketers. Because of its basis in individual social comparison, fashion cannot be controlled without undermining its ultimate purpose, which is the expression of individual identity. If self-identity were never in doubt and social comparison never took place, there would be no demand for fashion, and there would be no need or opportunity for style change. (1998: 35)

Cannon focuses on the phenomenon of fashion, that is the changing styles in dress, but does not explain whether the term that is equivalent to 'fashion' exists in traditional societies. The investigation of fashion as an institutionalized system in Chapter 3 will answer the question as to why fashion exists in some cities and cultures.

Flugel (1930) distinguishes between 'fixed' and 'modish' forms of dress. He suggests that fashion is linked to a particular type of social organization, particular type of society and culture, those of the West. Fixed costume changes slowly while modish costume changes very rapidly in time. For him, it is this latter type of costume which predominates in the Western world today, and which indeed (with certain important exceptions) has predominated there for several centuries; a fact that must be regarded as one of the most characteristic features of modern European civilization, since in other civilizations, both of the past and of the present, fashion seems to have played a very much more modest role (Flugel 1930: 130). Like Flugel, in separating fashion, as a process of continuous change, from short-term, ephemeral fads, Blumer (1969a), for example, largely removed fashion from the domain of traditional societies (see also Kawamura 2004).

Contemporary Sociological Studies of Fashion

Classical theorists gave mostly an intuitive and anecdotal observation of fashion providing no empirical evidence to support their theories. The significant shift over the twentieth century and into the twenty-first century is that contemporary scholars conduct empirical research for their studies of fashion.

Bourdieu (1984), a French sociologist, shares many of his views with classical contemporary discourse of fashion as imitation. He includes fashion within his theory of distinction-making. He uses the notion of taste as a marker that produces and maintains social boundaries, both between the dominant and dominated classes and within these groups. Thus taste is one of the key signifiers and elements of social identity. Bourdieu's interpretation of clothing and fashion lies within the framework of cultural taste and of class struggle. The bourgeoisie emphasizes the aesthetic value and the importance of the distinction between inside and outside, domestic and public while the working classes make a realistic and functional use of clothing, and they want 'value for money' and what will last. Fashion has a distinction function and also opposes the dominant and the dominated fractions, or the established and the challengers, given the equivalence between economic power. This reinforcement of the line between classes is best seen in a society where there is no one absolute authoritative power such as the aristocrats in the feudal age. Fashion reflects the advent of democracy in which the boundaries between classes have become less rigid.

Bourdieu (1984) uses a survey technique and draws upon two major surveys, undertaken in 1963 and 1967–8, of 1,217 subjects from Paris, Lille and a small provincial town, supplemented by a wide range of data from other surveys concerned with a range of topics. The empirical part of the book is concerned with the detailed explication of the lifestyle differences of differing class fractions. As far as taste in clothing is concerned, statistics are given on clothing purchases. Questions are asked on the quantity and the quality of the purchased items of clothing. As with his other studies of aspects of French society, Bourdieu explicitly states that this is not just a study of France. The model, he argues, is valid beyond the particular French case and, no doubt, for every stratified society.

Bell (1976[1947]) used much of Veblen's theoretical framework of the trickle-down theory of fashion. Bell sees the concept of social class as essential to an understanding of the 'mechanism of fashion.' His view is similar to that of Simmel, a much earlier writer on fashion who believed that fashion arose as a form of class differentiation in a relatively open class society. As noted earlier, Simmel saw fashion as a process involving a series of steps: an elite class seeks to set itself apart by its distinctive dress; the class just below it then adopts this distinctive dress in order to identify with the superior status of the class above it; then the next lower class copies the dress of the elite group indirectly by copying the dress of the class just below the elite; and as a result of this emulation, the elite are forced to devise a new form of distinguishing dress.

One of the few contemporary sociologists who refers to imitation, as classical sociologists have done, is Koenig, a German sociologist. Koenig (1973) reviews much of the earlier work on fashion, and the basic ideas provided by Tarde, Spencer and Simmel, and he postulates that imitation, starting from an initial triggering action, creates currents that cause uniform action among the masses. Some factors promote and some inhibit imitation. Connections with the subject of our imitation promote imitation. Prominent factors can be sympathy, admiration or respect for the wisdom or the position of the person we imitate. However, it is always necessary for a certain relationship to exist between the imitator and the imitated. From this fact, we derive the principle that imitation is by no means random; it occurs exclusively along already existing social connections; the person imitated can be either an equal or a superior. This non-randomness also implies that imitation does not by itself create social relationships, but is merely one of several symptoms as well as manifestations of already existing relationships. This principle is confirmed when we look at the other side of the problem, the inhibition of imitation. We feel the most intense aversion to imitating some other person whenever this person's way of acting and thinking appears strange or senseless to us.

On the other hand, Blumer (1969a) does not believe that a class differentiation model is valid in explaining fashion in contemporary society and replaces it with collective selection. While appreciating Simmel's contribution to the study of fashion which he uses to set off his own argument, Blumer argues that it is a parochial treatment, suited only to fashion in dress in seventeenth-, eighteenth-, and nineteenth-century Europe within a particular class structure. It does not fit the operation of fashion in our contemporary epoch with its many diverse fields and its emphasis on modernity. While not rejecting the power of the prestige of a wearer, he argues that one does not set the direction of fashion. Blumer takes a different perspective and argues:

> The efforts of an elite class to set itself apart in appearance take place inside of the movement of fashion instead of being its cause . . . The fashion mechanism appears not in response to a need of class differentiation and class emulation, but in response to a wish to be in fashion, to be abreast of what has good standing, to express new tastes which are emerging in a changing world. (1969a: 281)

Blumer (1969a) participated in the seasonal fashion shows in Paris and saw buyers and journalists selecting the styles which would eventually be presented for consumers. This is how he observed that fashion buyers are the unwitting surrogates of the fashion public. He said: 'It is not the prestige of the elite which makes the design fashionable but, instead, it is the suitability or potential fashionableness of the design which allows the prestige of the elite to be attached to it. The design has to correspond to the direction of incipient taste of the fashion consuming public' (1969a: 280).

Fashion as Collective Selection

The transformation of taste, of collective taste, results from the diversity of experience that occurs in social interaction. For Blumer, fashion is directed by consumer taste and it is a fashion designer's task to predict and read the modern taste of the collective mass. He is proposing a 'trickle-up' theory and situates consumers in the construction of fashion. But fashion encompasses more than consumers although they cannot be excluded from fashion.

Like Blumer, Davis (1992) rejects the class-differentiation model and argues that the model used by classical theorists is outdated because although what people wear and how they wear it can reveal much regarding their social standing, this is not all that dress communicates, and under many circumstances, it is by no means the most important thing communicated. He shares with Blumer the view that it is to the collective facets of our social identities that fashion addresses itself. His focus is a relationship between fashion/clothing and individual identity in modern society. According to Davis, as one's identity becomes increasingly multiple, the meaning of fashion also becomes increasingly ambivalent – a notion in line with postmodern thought. According to Davis:

> our social identities are rarely the stable amalgams we take them to be. Prodded by social and technological change, the biological decrements of the life cycle, visions of utopia, and occasions of disaster, our identities are forever in ferment, giving rise to numerous strains, paradoxes, ambivalences, and contradictions within ourselves. It is upon these collectively experienced, sometimes historically recurrent, identity instabilities that fashion feeds. (1992: 17)

However, if we concentrate only on the ambiguity of fashion as Davis suggests, it leaves nothing for sociologists to investigate. Ephemerality and ambiguity are the reasons why fashion is not taken seriously. It is the content of fashion that is constantly shifting, not the institutions (Kawamura 2004).

Fashion and Sociology of Culture

All the different perspectives of fashion discussed earlier, such as fashion as imitation, and fashion as an irrationally changing phenomenon often linked to women, neglect the systemic nature of fashion production, but they set the stage for the further discussion of fashion. A great deal of fashion writing in the mass media today drives away scholars, sociologists in particular, because they doubt the legitimacy of a subject that is believed to be ephemeral and without intellectual rationale. What sociologists of fashion can contribute to the project of cultural analysis is a focus on the institutions of fashion and the social relations among fashion professionals, the social differentiation between groups of designers, status of the designers, their ethnic heritage, and fashion systems worldwide. It is a sociology of culture that recognizes the importance of and pays much attention to the social-structural processes of cultural production and consumption. It operates with an understanding of social institutions and cultural symbols, which include activities and objects signified through culture. Thus it provides the interpretation of structural features of cultural life.

In the study of culture, it is necessary to understand not only technical processes and arrangement for manufacturing and distribution of cultural phenomena but also the culture through which the products are given meaning. We need to discover how products circulate, how they are given particular meanings in the context of a number of different production–consumption relationships. Thus I treat fashion as a cultural practice as well as a symbolic product. Culture is the means through which people create meaningful worlds in which to live. These cultural worlds are constructed through interpretations, experiences and activities whereby material is produced and consumed. In this book, I describe a set of organizations, individuals and routine organizational activities that both materially and symbolically produce items of fashion culture, some of which become popular and influential, most of which do not. This perspective locates culture in concrete social and cultural institutions.

Since, within the study of culture, fashion can be treated as a manufactured cultural object, sociologists who study fashion can learn much from sociologists analyzing other symbol-producing cultural institutions, such as art, science and religion. Cultural objects can be analyzed from both/either consumption and/or production perspectives. Likewise, fashion can be a matter of personal consumption and identity, and also a matter of collective production and distribution. Like sociologists of culture who focus on the production perspective of culture, such as the production of art culture, literary culture and gastronomic culture, I will discuss the production of fashion culture which is supported by the fashion system to which individuals, organizations and institutions belong.

Fashion is legitimate to study as a symbolic cultural object and as a manufactured thing produced in and by social organizations. Fashion is not visible or tangible and therefore uses clothing as a symbolic manifestation. The production of symbols places emphasis on the dynamic activity of institutions. Cultural institutions support the production of new symbols. Processes of production are themselves cultural phenomena in that they are combinations of meaningful practices that construct certain ways for individuals to conceive of and conduct themselves in an organizational context.

Whether fashion is art or not has been much debated, but it certainly follows what sociologists have postulated for the arts (Becker 1982; Bourdieu and Delsaut 1975; White and White 1993[1965]; Wolff 1983, 1993; Zolberg 1990). Those scholars who start from the premise that art should be contextualized in terms of place and time direct attention to the relation of the artist and artwork to extra-aesthetic considerations (Zolberg 1990). Bourdieu (1984) and Becker (1982) analyze the social construction of aesthetic ideas and values and focus on the processes of creation, production, institutions and organizations. In this perspective, a work of art is a process involving the collaboration of more than one actor and working through certain social institutions. Like art, fashion is social in character, has a social base and exists in a social context. Moreover, it involves large numbers of people. Like other social phenomena including art, fashion cannot be interpreted apart from its social context, and very few have attempted to look carefully at the organizational setting in which fashion is produced.

Fashion as a Manufactured Cultural Symbol

The sociology of culture represented most prominently by the study of arts organizations and institutions is known as 'the production-of-culture approach' and begins from the assumption that the production of cultural objects involves social cooperation, collective activities and groups. These cultural objects become a part of and contribute to culture. The production-of-culture approach is most useful in clarifying the rapid changes in popular culture where 'production' is our front and where the explanation of novelty and change is more pertinent than the explanation of stasis (Peterson 1976). There is no more apt an idea to study than fashion where novelty is the very key in defining the concept.

Commonalities found in social and not aesthetic factors make the study of fashion just as important as the study of fine art or classical music. Like art, fashion can be assimilated into the sociology of occupations and organization. In either case, the artist or the designer is dethroned as a genius whose creativity can only be appreciated rather than analyzed and replaced with a worker whose habits can be systematically investigated. In spite of the emphasis on the role of creative individuals, it is social groups that ultimately produce art, music, literature, television news and fashion as social phenomenon. These studies typically study, for instance, publishers' decision-making criteria in commercial publishing houses (Coser 1982), the role of the radio and record industries in relation to changes in the world of country music (Peterson 1997), or the gatekeeper role of commercial galleries in the New York art world (Szántó 1996). Other work has taken its departure from Becker's analysis (1982) which is devoted to the investigation of the social relations of cultural production, from composers and performers to instrument-makers, fundraisers and so on. Becker's work identifies the social hierarchies of art, its decision-making processes and aesthetic outcomes of these extra-aesthetic factors.

What is most significant in placing fashion and fashion designers within the sociology of culture and arts, is that neither the sociology of culture nor the sociology of arts treats the objects as the creation of an individual genius. This is the fundamental principle shared by sociology of fashion and sociology of culture and the arts. Studies of fashion and designers can draw much from Becker's studies on arts and artists and Peterson's study on the music industry and musicians. In opposition to the idea that cultural artifacts are simply the work of individual artists from whom they are then filtered to the public, Peterson (1976) stresses that the elements of culture are fabricated among occupational groups and within social mileux for whom symbol-system production is most self-consciously the center of activity. On the other hand, Becker (1982) reminds readers that the principle of his analysis is social organizational, not aesthetic, and he argues that the creation of works of art involves collective practices which are coordinated by shared conventions or rules and consensual definitions that were arrived at as various people formed, were attracted to and actively recruited to inhabit different 'art worlds.' For Becker, the cultural and social values of the art created the conditions for creative collaboration, which are deliberately invented by formal cultural organizations.

Ryan and Peterson (1982) illustrate an empirical case study of country music. They considered the work of a number of skilled specialists who have a part in shaping the final work as it goes through a series of stages which, superficially at least, resemble an assembly line. They followed the progress of country music songs along a decision chain of activities that involved writing, publishing, recording, marketing, manufacturing, release and consumption. At each stage they observed that a number of choices were confronted and a number of modifications might be made to the songs. Music was allowed to change as it passed along the chain. Thus music represents more than the sounds we hear just as fashion is more than what we wear. Ryan and Peterson argue that the making of country music is coordinated around the idea of a 'product image.' This involved the different people in the process, from studio producers to promotion people, using their judgment to shape 'a piece of work so that it is most likely to be accepted by decision makers at the next link in the chain' (Ryan and Peterson 1982). All the personnel involved in the chain were adopting a pragmatic, strategic and commercially oriented approach, organized around a 'product image,' which then enabled them to collaborate in a very practical way.

Such an approach draws heavily on the professional ideas of senior record company executives who often explain that their organizations work in these very terms – staff united with a shared, commercially defined goal, that is producing the image, which overrides personal or departmental divisions (Ryan and Peterson 1982). While music industry staff may have some notion of a 'product image' as a type of professional ideal, this idea may often be contested, challenged and transformed as a recording is produced, rather than acting simply as an organizing principle. While staff clearly had some notion of a 'product image,' there were a number of different ideas about the meaning of this 'product image' and how it should be pursued in practical terms.

However, producing culture does not simply involve making a product. Culture is not simply a product that is created, disseminated and consumed, but it is a product that is processed by organizational and macro-institutional factors. Today's designers place the strongest emphasis in recreating and reproducing their image, and the image that is projected through clothing is reflected on the designer's personal image as an individual. Both the fashion and music industries, in this sense, are image-making industries.

Although Becker does not use a term 'art system' – instead he uses 'art worlds' – my research has many parallels with his analysis. With the focus of sociologists on social structure and process, most of the writing on the sociology of the arts deals with the structure and activity of groups and institutions that handle art. Becker examines material, social and symbolic resources for the creation of meaningful cultural objects. He is not interested in what the final objects mean but makes an attempt to explain what is social about them. He focuses on the wide array of cooperative links between 'creators' and 'support personnel' necessary for the production of cultural objects. Critics, dealers and museum personnel, like everyone else in Becker's art worlds, simply do their jobs. Their special power in the world of art and the relationship of aesthetic stratification of culture to social hierarchy are not things Becker primarily pays attention to. He does not emphasize how such hierarchical considerations, both social and aesthetic, enter into the production process.

Unlike Becker's work, my analysis includes the stratification dimensions of producers of fashion, designers in particular, to understand social differences among those who design clothes in the system of fashion. Bourdieu's cultural analysis directs attention towards the stratification functions of cultural systems, that is, to the way social groups are identified by their cultural tastes or their abilities to create cultural institutions suited to members of their social strata. While Bourdieu is concerned with the differences between the groups who consume cultural symbols, I concentrate on the stratification within the occupational group of designers in Paris. Cultural stratification theory as represented by Bourdieu begins from the assumption that cultural differences and social attention to cultural differences are important sociologically because they are linked to fundamental patterns of social stratification, that is maintained by differences in the cultural attributes of people from different strata. The designers' position within the system of stratification determines the status of products they produce. At the same time, the designers' social status reflects on the that of their audience.

Furthermore, the production-of-culture perspective includes studies dealing with many different aspects of culture, and applies to studies of the arts, media and popular culture, market structures, and gatekeeping systems on the careers and activities of culture creators (Crane 1992). White and White's (1993[1965]) classic study of the emergence of Impressionist art in nineteenth-century France can also be treated within the production-of-culture framework. They found that the older academic art production system collapsed from inherent structural conditions, and Impressionist painters came in through the emerging art market developed by Parisian dealers and critics.

The production-of-culture perspective has been criticized for failing to pay attention to 'features of the art object itself,' tending towards empiricism and not locating specific institutions in the wider social context (Wolff 1993). It is also considered to be ahistorical and to lack explanatory power and critical sociological power (Wolff 1993: 31). However, it often produces very detailed, small-scale studies, and that helps us see the processes and institutions of artistic production in detail and deviate our attention from the material object of clothing and dress.

Conclusion

By observing the placement of fashion within different theoretical frameworks, we understand better what fashion means sociologically. Conceptions of fashion vary widely. Fashion can be treated as a form of social regulation or control, a hierarchy, a social custom, a social process and mores. Attempts to understand the dynamics of fashion have been mostly dominated by variants of imitation theory that start from the presumption that fashion is an essentially hierarchical phenomenon prescribed by some identifiable sartorial authority. Sartorial power is most often conceived as residing with some dominant social group or class whose decisions on what is fashionable are then emulated by successive layers of the social hierarchy. Imitation from below induces a pressure on social superiors to display their superiority by further sartorial refinement and innovation in order to distinguish themselves from their inferiors who have adopted their earlier styles. A potentially unending cycle of imitation and innovation is set up.

If early sociological work on fashion can best be analyzed through the concept of imitation, contemporary work is far too diverse to allow any such generalization. This is precisely because definitions and meanings of fashion have multiplied. Fashion discourse has spread to various academic disciplines and has become overtly interdisciplinary. In the next chapter, I will explain my approaches to fashion by integrating additional contemporary discourse as well as empirical studies on fashion that laid the foundation of Fashion-ology. Studying fashion from a systemic point of view provides a different approach to fashion and answers many questions such as the feminization of fashion and the Eurocentric view of the origin of fashion.

3

Fashion as an Institutionalized System

As indicated in the review of the classical and contemporary discourse and various empirical studies of fashion in the previous chapters, fashion is commonly attached to clothes and appearances, and therefore, visual documents are frequently used as evidence because many writers treat fashion as a material object. Thus, it becomes difficult or almost impossible to separate fashion and clothing. I provide a different approach to fashion, that is fashion as an institutionalized system. I align my investigation primarily with Crane's several empirical studies on the fashion industry and designers in Paris, New York and London (1997a, 1997b, 2000) which are used as the point of departure from where I can start and narrow my observation. Davis's (1992) discussion on fashion as a system as well as the literature on sociology of the arts and culture (Becker 1982; White and White 1993[1965]; Wolff 1983, 1993; Zolberg 1990) have also been used to understand fashion as a cultural symbol as noted in the previous chapter. Barthes's semiotic analysis (1967) makes us aware of the clothing system and helps us develop the concept of an institutionalized system with the concept of and the practice of fashion.

In this chapter, I will give an overview of fashion as a system and the theoretical underpinnings of Fashion-ology and explain how fashion can be studied empirically as an institution or an institutionalized system in which individuals related to fashion, including designers among many other fashion professionals, engage in activities collectively, share the same belief in fashion and participate together in producing and perpetuating not only the ideology of fashion but also fashion culture which is sustained by the continuous production of fashion. The production process of fashion must be clearly distinguished from that of clothing because clothing does not immediately convert into fashion. Fashion-ology mainly discusses the production of fashion, but it does not preclude consumption of fashion because production and consumption are, as we will see in Chapter 6, complementary.

As Finkelstein notes (1996: 6), it would be misleading to think of fashion only in regard to clothing since there are other considerations which take the idea of fashion beyond material goods. Similarly, Koenig (1973: 40) states that we must destroy the widely held prejudice that fashion is only concerned with the outer cover of the human being in dress, jewelry and ornaments. Since it is a general social institution, it affects and shapes individuals and society as a whole. Therefore, those discussions of fashion that focus exclusively on the study of or the history of dress are inadequate (Koenig 1973: 40), and the study of fashion as a system or Fashion-ology entails a different analytical framework.

Theoretical Framework of Fashion-ology

Fashion-ology integrates both micro and macro levels of social theories, that is symbolic interactionism and structural functionalism, because we focus on a macro-sociological analysis of the social organization of fashion as well as a micro-interactionist analysis of designers and individuals involved in producing fashion. There are many interpretations of fashion, and I add another perspective to it by viewing it as an institutionalized system. This is unlike those approaches to fashion which focus on styles of dress and clothing. There is a lack of attention to the social context of the institutional development of fashion, and that is what Fashion-ology attempts to address. The sociological study of fashion can expose many of the extra-aesthetic elements involved in aesthetic judgment and functions served by the institutions of fashion.

A structural functional perspective of fashion includes the production, distribution and consumption of goods and services which are intimately related. A society cannot distribute what it does not produce and cannot produce without distributing. In addition, the capacity to produce is greatly influenced by the pattern of distribution that motivates the members of society and distributes skills and opportunities. This analysis is an attempt to establish causal connections between standardized, repetitive patterns of social life and their consequences. In Merton's formulations of a structural-functional perspective (1957), functions or dysfunctions can be attributed only to standardized items such as social roles, institutional patterns and social structure, and 'standardized' means patterned and repetitive. This means that single events cannot be made the subject of functional analysis. This is applicable to the institutions of fashion that are found in cities where fashion culture is found. Fashion shows, which are organized at least twice a year and are controlled by trade associations, are used as the means to mobilize those who are involved in the production and distribution of fashion.

Moreover, Merton's distinction between manifest and latent functions further clarifies functional analysis (1957). Manifest functions are the consequences people observe or expect while latent functions are the consequences that are neither recognized nor intended. While Parsons (1968) emphasized the manifest functions of social behavior, Merton pays particular attention to the latent functions of things and the increased understanding of society that functionalist analysis can bring by uncovering them. The distinction forces sociologists to go beyond the reasons individuals give for their actions or for the existence of customs and institutions. For example, Merton (1957) cites Veblen's analysis of conspicuous consumption and explains that the latent function of conspicuous consumption is the enhancement of one's status. One of the purposes of fashion shows is to show new styles to journalists, editors and buyers. But the unintended consequence of those events is that the site of mobilization confirms that that is where fashion emerges from. That contributes to adding value to clothing and transforming it into fashion although this happens only in people's minds. In this way, fashion culture continues and is sustained. In turn, it attracts designers to the city which everyone believes is the fashion capital, and fashion survives and the city remains influential.

Functional analysis should also specify the mechanisms or processes by which consequences occur and alternative arrangements by which functions can be achieved. Functional alternatives are limited by structural constraints. A process or mechanism that has consequences in one structural context may not have the same consequences in another. Thus, merely organizing a fashion show does not make a city the fashion center. Paris, in particular, has historically been making efforts to maintain its image so that the city continues to be the fashion capital.

Structural functionalists explain that Sociology should only be concerned with social structures which determine the characteristics and actions of individuals, whose agency or special characteristics become unimportant. Durkheim was an early exponent of this position. Functionalists often adopt this view, being concerned simply with the functional relationships between social structures. We must also investigate the conditions in which the designer is acclaimed as talented and gifted. By participating in the fashion-related events, already known designers confirm their status and reputation and the new ones seek to be discovered by the gatekeepers who represent major magazines and newspapers.

In contrast to macro approaches to fashion, symbolic interactionists advocate the method that looks at the processes by which individuals define the world from the inside and at the same time identify their world of objects. The various techniques utilized in this phase are directly observing (both participant and non-participant), interviewing people, listening to conversations and to radio and television, reading local newspapers and periodicals, securing life-history accounts, reading letters and diaries and consulting public records. One must attain a close and full familiarity with the world one is examining. Blumer's major contribution to symbolic interactionism has been his elaboration on methodology of symbolic interactionism, and he showed that, unlike functionalism, symbolic interactionism is not a deductive theory that begins with a set of hypothesis. He used the method to study fashion (1969b).

Symbolic interactionists are primarily concerned with explaining individuals' particular decisions and actions and with demonstrating the impossibility of explaining these by predetermined rules and external forces. Most of the analysis is of small-scale interpersonal relationships, and individuals are viewed as active constructors of their own conduct who interpret, evaluate, define and map out their own action, rather than as passive beings who are impinged upon by outside forces. Symbolic interactionism also stresses the processes by which the individual makes decisions and forms opinions. One can interview designers and fashion professionals in investigating their relationship with the fashion organization and institutions and how they interact with other fashion professionals in the same institutional and individual networks.

An important debate in sociological theory concerns the relationship between individuals and social structure. The debate revolves around the problem of how structures determine what individuals do, how structures are created, and what are the limits, if any, on individuals' capacities to act independently of structural constraints; what are the limits, in other words, on human agency. Wolff explains the connection: 'The artist, as cultural producer, then, has a place in the sociology or art. It is no longer necessary for sociological analysis to have to choose whether to give priority to "action" or to "structure," or to argue about voluntarism or determinism ... we have to operate with a model which posits the mutual interdependence of structure and agency' (1993: 138).

As we look at how the institutions of fashion function and the individuals involved in fashion participate in those institutions, the system of fashion becomes much clearer, and at the same time, we can understand how the two are interdependent and interrelated.

Fashion as a Myth Supported by the System

The primary focus of Fashion-ology is, therefore, an institutionalized system of fashion. To analyze fashion as a system, we must look for its systemic characteristics, the kinds of workers it involves and the tasks each worker does. Fashion is a system of institutions, organizations, groups, producers, events and practices, all of which contribute to the making of fashion, which is different from dress or clothing. It is the structural nature of the system that affects the legitimation process of designers' creativity. A systemic differentiation can be made between clothes and fashion which are two independent, autonomous entities. As noted earlier, fashion is a manufactured cultural symbol in an institutionalized system. Institutional factors in the social process of the making of a designer must also be examined. Although designers play an important role in the system, we should not neglect other fashion-related occupational groups in the system, such as journalists and publicists among many others. Strictly speaking, Fashion-ology does not directly include the discussion of the production process of and the details of the garments since they are included in the study of clothing and dress.

When I say that fashion is an ideology, I do not mean in a Marxist aesthetics sense, locating the works of the designers in the social and political environment. An ideology is a myth, and it may be defined as beliefs, attitudes and opinions all of which can be tightly or loosely related. Ideology constitutes any set of beliefs, and whether they are true or false is not relevant for it to exist. All beliefs are socially determined in some way or another although there is no assumption that any one factor is more important or more true.

Fashion as a myth has no scientific and concrete substance. The function of myth is essentially cognitive, namely to account for the fundamental conceptual categories of the mind. It embodies collective experiences and represents the collective conscience, and this is how the myth continues. While traditional anthropology was concerned with the study of myths in primitive society, the structural analysis of myth has also been applied to modern industrial societies. For instance, Barthes (1964) treats myths as a system of communications, consisting not only of written discourses, but also the products of cinema, sport, photography, advertising and television. Likewise, social institutions and practices construct the fashion myth. Understanding fashion as a system helps us demystify the belief in fashion and also analyze 'the mysterious dictates of the fashion capital Paris' (Flugel 1930: 147). Flugel remarks:

Fashion, we have been brought up to believe (and generations of writers in the myriad of journals have contributed to this belief), is a mysterious goddess, whose decrees it is our duty to obey rather than to understand; for indeed, it is implied, these decrees transcend all ordinary human understanding. We know not why they are made, or how long they will endure, but only that they must be followed; and that the quicker the obedience the greater is the merit. (1930: 137)

It was always the French kings, queens and aristocrats who initiated fashion trends which subsequently trickled down to the masses and spread to other parts of Europe. Latest fashions were found in Paris, and foreigners and Parisians make pilgrimages to the source of Paris fashions (Steele 1988: 27).

A fashion-ological approach to fashion can also provide the answer to the fickleness of fashion. Laver explained fashion's irrationality and super-ficial tendencies as follows:

'pleasures of vicissitude' adds to the enjoyment of life. Fads, crazes, fashion moods and fashion follies within the fashion of the day bring short lived amusement. People who always do the same things and wear the same clothes, are themselves bored and make them boring for others. Every fashion is in existence for a certain period of time and nobody knows exactly when or why its popularity suddenly arises and then almost as quickly as it came, fades away. (1950: 66)

An empirical study on fashion as a system shows the distinction between clothing and fashion and that fashion is not created in a vacuum. The differences between the two can be clearly drawn as follows (Kawamura 2004: 1):

Clothing is material production while fashion is symbolic production. Clothing is tangible while fashion is intangible. Clothing is a necessity while fashion is an excess. Clothing has a utility function while fashion has a status function. Clothing is found in any society or culture where people clothe themselves while fashion must be institu-tionally constructed and culturally diffused. A fashion system operates to convert clothing into fashion that has a symbolic value and is manifested through clothing.

In explaining the labeling process of deviance, Becker (1982) says that social definitions create reality, and therefore, sociologists need to ask, in the same manner, who is entitled to label things as fashion or fashionable. We need only observe which members of the fashion system are treated as capable of doing that. Some occupy institutional positions which allow them to decide what will be acceptable and fashionable. As far as French fashion is concerned, it is the members of the trade organization.[1]

Based on White and White's study (1993[1965]) on the French Impressionists and Becker's analysis of the art world (1982), fashion can be examined as a system composed of various institutions. These institutions together reproduce the image of fashion and perpetuate the culture of fashion in major fashion cities, such as Paris, New York, London and Milan. My empirical study (Kawamira 2004) of French fashion indicates that fashion as a system first emerged in Paris in 1868 with the institutionalization of exclusive custom-made clothes known as Haute Couture. The system consists of a number of subsystems comprised of a network of designers, manufacturers, wholesalers, public relations officers, journalists and advertising agencies. The fashion industry is not simply concerned with the production of adequate or pleasant clothing but is concerned with the production of new stylistic innovations that satisfy the image of fashion. Similarly, in the case of the art world, it consists of artists, producers, museum directors, museum-goers, theater-goers, reporters for newspapers, critics for publications of all sorts, art historians, art theorists, philosophers of art among others, and they keep the machinery of the art world working and thereby provide for its continuing existence (Dickie quoted in Becker 1982: 150).

Fashion-ology suggests that any item of clothing is capable of being appreciated and can be turned into fashion. Not every attempt to label something fashion may be successful, but there is nothing more to making something fashion than christening or legitimating it. It is the institutions of fashion that do that. The designers must be recognized by other participants in the cooperative activities through which their works are produced and consumed by others.

Different Approaches to Fashion Systems

I will first explain different approaches to a fashion system before introducing a fashion-ological approach to fashion since many writers of fashion and/or dress refer to the term 'fashion system' although what they mean and their definitions may vary. Some define a fashion system by separating it from a clothing manufacturing system while others use the term in a very loose way and make no distinction between the two systems.

For Leopold (1993: 101), a fashion system takes part in the clothing production process. A fashion system is the inter-relationship between highly fragmented forms of production and equally diverse and often volatile patterns of demand. She argues that fashion incorporates dual concepts of fashion as a cultural phenomenon, and as an aspect of manufacturing with the accent on production technology. She emphasizes the important role of clothing production and its history in creating fashion and dismisses the argument, unlike Blumer (1969a), that consumer demand determines the creation of fashion.

While McCraken demonstrates that the language–product comparison is unsound, Barthes (1967) and Lurie[2] (1981) use linguistics systems in parallel to fashion systems to explain fashion and clothing. They treat the two the same or as interchangeable concepts. Clothing can be used as a metaphor. This has been criticized by many fashion writers as clothing and fashion cannot be used for communication as accurately as the language we speak. Such approach to fashion and dress is very limited and does not expand further. Both of them base their semiotic analysis of clothing and fashion on structural linguistics, initiated by Ferdinand de Saussure (1972). Saussure's theory of signs known as semiology helps us in making the distinction between clothing and fashion. Despite the title of the book *The Fashion System* (1967), Barthes is not talking about a fashion system but a clothing system. One can use his complex analysis in finding a distinction between the fashion system and the clothing system. The clothing system teaches us how to wear garments and what to wear in specific social and cultural contexts because each context has different social meanings. There are rules about what Western clothes must look like. We have learned through socialization that a shirt usually has two sleeves or a pair of pants has two legs. Similarly, there are conventions that we take for granted as far as stylistic coordination is concerned. These conventions are unwritten laws or folkways in Sumner's term, and these sartorial conventions make a clothing system. The standard clothing system for Western clothes helps us see the deviations from that system although the clothing system does not explain the fashion system.

Roach and Musa (1980) make a distinction between a simple fashion system and a complex fashion system, that is a system in modern society. They refer to, for example, the fashion system among the Tiv of Nigeria, in which types of scars used for beautification change from generation to generation (1980: 20). In this fashion system, scar designs and techniques are devised, copied, popularized, abandoned and replaced by others on the basis of person-to-person contact. A simple fashion system is found in small-scale, pre-modern societies. On the other hand, a system can be as complex as that in so-called fashion cities, such as Paris, New York and Milan, and this system involves thousands of people, such as designers, assistant designers, stylists, manufacturers of textiles, garments, buttons, and cosmetics, wholesalers, retail buyers, publicists, advertisers and fashion photographers among many other fashion professionals.

Similarly, Blumer (1969a) also uses the term 'fashion system.' He analyzes the functions of fashion as a social mechanism, particularly its integrating functions within industrial society, where a highly intricate fashion system has developed. He does not use dress or clothing to describe the nature of the twentieth-century fashion systems, but adds that dress is only one aspect of life that fashion affects. Blumer has contributed a theory of fashion appropriate to contemporary mass society. He sees the fashion system as a complex means for facilitating orderly change within a mass society no longer able to provide identity and maintain order via social custom.

Davis (1992) also distinguishes clothing from fashion systems although he does not elaborate on the clothing system in particular. He said: 'the core image of an innovating center, archetypically Paris with its highly developed haute couture establishment, surrounded by sociologically sedi-mented and differentially receptive bands of fashion consumers . . . remained securely in place' (1992: 200). His usage means to point to the more or less established practices of the complex institutions, such as design, display, manufacture, distribution and sales, that process fashion as they make their way from creators to consumers. However, Davis does not elaborate on the internal structure of this system, and the processes that creators and consumers go through and the roles they play within the system.

Koenig consciously separates fashion from dress and clothing. Fashion is not only about what we wear and consume. Koenig states:

> We . . . distinguish between the socio-psychological, structural form of fashion as a social regulator in its own right and its various and forever variable contents. This also implies that we take fashion completely seriously as an independent social institution . . . This approach to fashion also means that, unlike the many fashion writers in the daily papers, journals, illustrated weeklies and magazines, we do not want to pronounce judgment on various fashions. As we have already pointed, our real invention is to analyse the 'system of fashion.' This also means keeping a certain distance from the fashion of the day one will succumb to it and automatically be caught in the dialectical whirlpool of its infinite variations. (1973: 38–9)

Craik also employs the term 'fashion system':

> While western elite designer fashion constitutes one system, it is by no means exclu-sive nor does it determine all other systems. Just as fashion systems may be periodised from the late Middle Ages until the present . . . so too contemporary fashion systems may be recast as an array of competing and inter-meshing systems cutting across western and non-western cultures. (1994: 6)

Craik's usage of the fashion system implies that there was a fashion system in the Middles Ages. I argue that clothing systems are found in Western and non-Western societies but not fashion systems. Fashion became institutionalized for the first time in mid-nineteenth-century France although fashion as a practice was evident in France during the reign of Louis XIV. Entwistle (2000) also points out that a specific system of dress originates in the West although her emphasis is on the connections between the body, fashion and dress.

On the other hand, McCraken (1988) argues that imitation became possible due to the advent of a fashion system, but at the same time, there was the loss of symbols, and with this loss, there was the drive to create more innovation. He indicates different values emerging with the arrival of the fashion system and the end of patina as a means of controlling status expression. The system enabled status misrepresentations and deceptions, and it deprived the elite groups of their privilege, and they were now forced continually to adopt new fashions to recreate the distinction patina had previously supplied them. They were now, in a more than figurative sense of the phrase, the prisoners of fashion (McCraken 1988: 40).

The assignment of a new status meant that one could turn income into status immediately and one did not have to wait over many generations to make an object a patina. This allowed the status system to incorporate the upwardly mobile and also allowed it to reward those who had proven themselves worthy of advancement. It also encouraged new mobility and the recognition of ability. The patina strategy had served the cause of relative rigidity, fixity, and immobility, and it was the fashion system that served the cause of mobility (McCraken 1988: 40–1). Therefore, for McCraken, a fashion system began long before my definition of a fashion system (Kawamura 2004) that began in 1868 when the structural relationship between a designer/couturier and a client was reversed.

I began my empirical research (Kawamura 2004) from where Davis left off, exploring the institutions within the fashion system in France which, according to my analysis, is the prototype of the system in general. Davis's analysis of the fashion system (1992) was used as a point of departure. I treat fashion as an institutional system, that is a persistent network of beliefs, customs and formal procedures which together form an articulated social organization with an acknowledged central purpose (White and White 1993[1965]). No matter what its size, a fashion system seems to have certain basic features. The minimum requirement is a network of people that includes those who introduce or propose changes in dress and those who adopt at least a portion of the proposed changes. The proposers and adopters in this network must be in communication with each other, either directly on a person-to-person basis or indirectly as through mass communication.

The Beginning of the Fashion System

Unraveling the mysteries of the evolving fashion system that reached out both nationally and internationally became a challenge (Roach-Higgins and Eicher 1973: 28). There are conditions necessary for a fashion system to exist and operate, and those are a multi-level open class system, within which more than one class is able to participate in fashion change in dress, and the possibility of mobility from one class to the next; and the presence of competition between at least two classes. In addition, change and novelty must be positively valued within the cultural group in question. If stability rather than change is highly valued, the rapid replacement of one form of dress for another, as fashion change implies, is unlikely to be perceived as desirable. Then fashion does not develop.

It is not easy to specify a point in time in the history of Western dress when a fashion system can be said to have begun. Roach-Higgins (1995) explains that visible, short-term changes in some elements of dress likely date back to whenever humans living in groups produced a surplus in economic resources and were, therefore, able to make choices in dress that went beyond the absolute minimum for ensuring physical survival. If variations in dress elements were devised by one or more members of the group and consequently adopted by others for a limited time, then we could say that the fundamental idea of a fashion system existed. Scholars generally recognize the fourteenth century as a time when workers in costume crafts, merchants, and eager customers, both an aristocracy and a wealthy bourgeoisie, clearly portrayed the kinds of social behavior associated with fashion, behavior from which the highly complex fashion system of the twentieth and twenty-first centuries has evolved (Roach-Higgins 1995: 395–6).

Bell (1976[1947]) coined the term 'micro-fashions' to recognize the existence of the relatively minor types of fashion change that may have taken place in the ancient civilizations of China, Rome, Byzantine and Egypt. He hypothesized a beginning for the Western fashion system as early as the time of the first crusades, and he asserted that during the 700 years that separated the first crusade in 1096 from the French Revolution, fashion accelerated while slowly gathering momentum.

Boucher (1987[1967]) is more specific and associates the beginning of an identifiable Western fashion system with the fourteenth century. We favor use of this date since a noticeable acceleration in the rate of change in dress had taken place by this time. This acceleration can be associated with the accumulated influence of a number of factors. These factors include: specialization in crafts associated with textile and apparel production; decline of the feudal system; and development of a court system associated with a principality or state, and growing international interdependencies that required intricate economic and political strategies in defense of national interests. This is also the beginning of Western dress. The fashion system provided the means whereby unique features of Western dress could be developed and distributed.

It is assumed that a fashion system emerged with the phenomenon of fashion, and therefore, they are synonymous. In defining a fashion system, as we noted earlier, the minimum requirements for its existence are someone who produces a fashion in dress and someone who consumes it; this concept accurately depicts the self-perpetuating nature of the fashion system.

In societies characterized by an elaborate division of labor, the development of a complex system of interdependent, specialized roles for accomplishing the designing, producing, distributing and consuming of dress is possible. In Kawamura (2004), the fashion phenomenon is separated from a fashion system, that is the modern system that began in 1868 with the institutionalization of fashion.

Fashion Production as Collective Activity

Clothing production and fashion production are both collective activities which require large numbers of people to produce the finished product. While clothing production manufactures items of garments, fashion production perpetuates the belief in fashion. Therefore, the processes and institutions that they go through are separate. Clothing production involves the actual manufacturing process of the material clothing. On the other hand, fashion production involves those who help construct the idea of fashion. Furthermore, treating fashion as a collective product is a broader task which refers to aspects of cultural production which do not feature in the immediate making of the work. Although fashion is not about clothing, without it, fashion cannot exist. They are not mutually inclusive nor are they mutually exclusive.

There is a clear division of labor among those who produce a garment. Just as painters depend on manufacturers for canvas, stretchers, paint, and brushes, dealers, collectors, and museum curators for exhibition space and

financial support, and on critics and aestheticians for the rationale for
what they do (Becker 1982: 13), thread manufacturers work with the
textile manufactures to produce textiles that will be selected, bought and
used by apparel manufacturers. The fashion designers work in the center
of a network of cooperating people, all of whose work is essential to the
final outcome. Fashion designers at the apparel firms work with assistant
designers, sample cutters, sample-makers, production pattern-makers and
then factories to finalize the garments. Trimmings and button suppliers are
also involved. Those individuals are indispensable for the execution of the
garments, but they are different from fashion producers. For the garment
to be appreciated, accepted and legitimated as fashion, it has to go through
a different process and mechanism. Similarly, there is a group of people,
whom I call fashion professionals, who make a contribution to not only the
production but also to gatekeeping and distribution of fashion.

As noted earlier, change is the essence of fashion, and therefore, as
Roach-Higgins notes, awareness of change by members of a collectivity is
a requisite for fashion (1985: 394). Their collective recognition, acceptance
and use of a particular form of dress, which they eventually replace with
another form, makes it a fashion. Fashion is a social regulating system in
its own right and differs from other regulating systems (such as those of
habit, custom, convention, morality, and the law) only in degree, not in
essence (Roach-Higgins and Eicher 1973: 31–2). In a society where change
in cultural forms is very slow – taking several generations or even centuries
– fashion is not a social reality; for members of the society, the collectivity,
do not recognize and consciously share the experience of change, let alone
promote it. If changeability is an integral part of a fashion phenomenon,
there is fashion in the system of Japanese kimonos or the system of Indian
saris. However, non-Western ethnographical case studies of the way people
dress often use the term 'dress,' 'cultural/ethnic dress' or 'costume,' rather
than 'fashion' because fashion is not only about change, but an institutionalized, systematic change produced by those who are authorized to
implement it. That kind of fashion system is found, at least for now, only
in the West. Without a system that includes a diffusion mechanism, any
style of dress is confined within its own system of clothing. There is a
whole network of people involved in clothing production and fashion
production. The tasks and individuals involved in clothing production are
different from those in fashion production.

Empirical Study: the French System as a Prototype

I argue that fashion systems exist only in specific types of cities where fashion is structurally organized. Drawing on these writers' notion of fashion as a system, I apply that concept to my understanding of the larger spectrum of fashion; that is the system that produces fashion designers, who in turn, along with other fashion professionals, perpetuate the culture of fashion. In my analysis, I employ the term 'fashion system' to describe organizations, institutions and individuals interacting with one another and to legitimate fashion designers and their creativity. The term does not describe the process of sewing clothes, which belongs to a separate kind of system, that is the clothing or manufacturing system. However, one cannot understand fashion without referring to clothes, and analysis of the designers' designs and styles is inevitable.

If the essence of fashion is mutability (Delpierre 1997), then how is this mutability or change brought about? Is there a logic behind continuous change or is it a natural phenomenon? Does change occur naturally, irrationally and irregularly? How does a style become fashion? The change has been systematically produced and institutionally conducted, and will continue to be if any fashion center chooses to maintain its hegemony. There is an interplay among fashion as a concept, a practice and a system. Becker explains the sociological perspective of art worlds:

> All artistic work, like all human activity, involves the joint activity of a number, often a large number, of people. Through their cooperation, the art work we eventually see or hear comes to be and continues to be ... The existence of art worlds, as well as the way their existence affects both the production and consumption of art works, suggests sociological approach to the arts. It is not an approach that produces aesthetic judgments, although that is a task many sociologists of art have set for themselves. It produces, instead, an understanding of the complexity of the cooperative networks through which art happens. (1982: 1)

We need to think of the activities that must be carried out for any work to appear as it finally does. In order for a garment to take some physical form, it has to go through the manufacturing process of the garment.

The French fashion trade organization plays a pivotal role within this system and has been instrumental in creating institutions that control the mobilization process of fashion professionals and organize fashion events and activities in Paris. Kawamura (2004) placed this trade organization at the core of her empirical analysis and elaborated the institutional network among organizations and individuals, as well as and examining the structural conditions influencing the decision of gatekeepers in the system of fashion. Fashion is very much the product of a chain of a great many individual decisions made by people interconnected within the various niches in the industry.

My case studies of Japanese designers in Paris[3] (2004) show how they destroyed the traditional Western clothing system and invented a new system while remaining within the traditional fashion system that is the French establishment. Clothes and fashion are two separate sociological concepts and systems, because the concept of fashion encompasses more than clothes. The French fashion system consists of different organizations with a hierarchy among those who design clothes: Haute Couture, Prêt-à-Porter for women and Prêt-à-Porter for men. Entries into these organizations are exclusive and difficult. The more exclusive the inclusion becomes, the more valuable the membership is.

Haute Couture was not simply a group of fashion houses, but a network of sub-contractors and suppliers who make all the hats, the gloves, the stockings, the corsets, the shoes, the handbags, the jewelry, the buckles, the belts and the buttons. There are the embroiderers, the make-up artists and the hairdressers in addition to all the representatives of the textile companies. They are also considered exclusive as they cater not only to ordinary designers but 'couturiers.'

One can look at other fashion systems in major fashion cities, London, New York, Milan and Tokyo, and make comparisons among them to investigate the differences and the similarities. The extent to which every fashion organization centralizes or decentralizes its authority of fashion can be researched. There is an unofficial couture group in Italy which is not acknowledged as a legitimate organization but which may have contributed in initiating the fashion organization for ready-to-wear, and not for custom-made clothes, similar to that of the French. Every fashion center has a trade organization, but the one in New York does not make its membership as exclusive as that in Paris. Organization is the key factor in the process of institutionalizing, and at the same time it is part of structuring cultural industry. It will be worthwhile to further investigate the role that the French government plays in maintaining the French hegemony of fashion, Haute Couture in particular, through, for instance, the apprenticeship system, loan structure and pricing of exclusive garments. Within the larger context, connections among other types of organizations, such as art, music or literary organizations, can be made because the comparisons bring out distinct points about fashion. Moreover, key players and key relations within each organization and system of fashion have to be examined.

The Institutionalization of French Fashion

Institutions provide the means and context through which elites exercise power. Fashion professionals become powerful and dominant through the control of major social institutions. Extraordinary centralization of power allows control over many people and resources. The actions of these institutions and the decisions of fashion professionals in Paris have extensive consequences. The French fashion system has autonomous power on a global scale, and it works to maintain its hegemony.

The institutional arrangements give advantages to some groups over others and reinforce the hierarchical structure among designers. Given that different groups within society are affected differently by social arrangements, designers' participation in the system affects their economic, social and cultural capital (Bourdieu 1984). Unlike Karl Marx, who traced all power relations back to the means of production, that is, economic capital, Bourdieu argues that there are three fundamental types of capital. *Economic capital* involves command over economic resources. *Social capital* commands relationships, networks of influence and support into which individuals can tap by virtue of their social position. *Cultural capital* explains the way in which both tastes and perceptions of what is beautiful or valuable, and social groups are ranked in society. Using cultural capital, according to Bourdieu (1984), the elites constantly distance themselves from the non-elites. Economic, social and cultural capital are the objects and the weapons of a competitive struggle between different groups and/or among individuals within the group. There is social and cultural reproduction and the fluidity over time of the system. Admission into the French fashion system grants both social capital and economic capital that separate the elite designers from the non-elites outside the system, that is, designers of mass-produced apparel. Designers fight over these resources, which may eventually lead to economic capital. Furthermore, how designers perform within the system affects their socio-cultural position in France and overseas, and the possibility of transforming their name into a symbolic trademark valid worldwide. Designers need to earn *symbolic capital* for their products for those consumers who wish to share that capital to differentiate themselves from those with whom they do not wish to identify. For Bourdieu (1984), 'symbolic capital' is essentially economic or cultural capital that is acknowledged and recognized, and then tends to reinforce the power relations which constitute the structure of social space. The symbolic value of goods is realized whenever people engage in consumption and thereby express their social identity. The French fashion system first provides designers the symbolic capital and then allows them to convert that symbolic capital into economic capital. Recognition that groups participate in social arrangements that put them at an advantage suggests the importance of the domination of some groups of designers in Paris. Therefore, acceptance by the system places the designer within the system of stratification.

Conclusion

The hierarchical structure of fashion which produces the authoritative status of designers, sounds inflexible, but in fact it is democratic and fluid. Fashion as an institution produces hierarchy among all makers of clothes by adding social, economic, cultural and symbolic capital to clothes, which are then transformed into luxury, elite clothes. Luxury clothes are meaningful only in relation to non-luxury clothes, but in modern capitalist societies anyone can obtain luxury clothes in less expensive ways. The democratization of luxury is increasingly allowing people to obtain luxury items. The motivation to attain is based on the desire to make a slight difference with others because luxury items provide a sense of superiority as an image and added values are attached to them.

The success of the French system in recruiting designers, institutionalizing fashion production and creating hierarchies among designers contributed to the international dominance of Paris. In this chapter, I have outlined the system of fashion production and showed how the fashion system in France is instrumental in producing fashion. The system institutionalizes the recognition process of members of the organization, fashion show schedules, fashion gatekeepers, government support, the nurturing of young designers, among other things, which are all indispensable for Paris to continue as the fashion capital. Any activity of a creative character may be recognized as artistic as a result of social and cultural factors. The judgment as 'creative' by a person of sufficient prestige and standing requires such conditions.

Short-term success does not guarantee enduring reputation. Having a fashion show every season is one of the tactics to maintain reputation in the world of French fashion. Failing to continue a show means that one will be excluded from the official list of the designers. The exclusion from the list means the loss of the French trade organization's recognition. Eventually, the loss of their recognition is equivalent to the loss of the status as a designer.

4

Designers: The Personification of Fashion

Designers are undoubtedly key figures in the production of fashion and play an important role in the maintenance, reproduction and dissemination of fashion. They are at the forefront in the field since their participation in the fashion system determines their status and reputation. Without designers, clothes do not become fashion. Although it is important to remember that they are not the only players, and they could not produce fashion by themselves without the collaboration of other fashion professionals and producers, as discussed in Chapter 5, designers are and must be portrayed as 'stars' in the production of fashion. With stars, the fashion form shines in all its glory. Designers personify fashion and their designs objectify fashion. Thus designers and clothing are inseparable from the notion of fashion. Many are involved in the production processes in creating the finished product, that is the finished item of clothing, and produce the label of fashion. Clothing that they design and make does not automatically turn into fashion. At that stage, they are producing clothing and not fashion. They make clothes but also produce fashion. Their job is to design clothes but that is only the manifest function of the designer. The designers personify 'fashion' that is timely, up-to-date and considered desirable. Because designing fashion is not a licensed occupation and designers can be self-claimed, legitmation in one way or another becomes crucial.

This chapter explores how designers are included in the studies of fashion, the link between designers' creativity and social structure, the star system that has personified 'fashion' since the time of the couturiers Charles Frederick Worth and Paul Poiret, and the hierarchical positions that the designers occupy within the fashion system.

Designers in the Studies of Fashion

None of the writers discuss the role that designers or creators of fashion play in producing fashion although the designers as we know today were already prominent at the turn of the twentieth century. Fashion design was never considered a legitimate occupation, and traditionally the attention was always on the upper-class women who wore luxury clothes.

Fashion has always been analyzed from the perspective of those who are adopting or consuming fashion because prior to the institutionalization, fashion emerged out of the upper-class men and women, and thus the producer and consumer of fashion shared the same origin. Those who initiated trends wore the latest, fashionable clothes. Designing as an occupation is a modern phenomenon that began with the institutionalized system of fashion in France in 1868, as discussed in Chapter 3. Fashion designated what elites wore. This presumption has faded with social change and democratization. Fashion is no longer only a trickle-down process coming from top to bottom as Tarde (1903) and others (Simmel 1957[1904]; Veblen 1957[1899]) argued but has also become a 'trickle-across' process as Spencer (1966[1896]) suggested in explaining competitive imitation or even a 'trickle-up' or 'bubble-up' process as Blumer (1969a, 1969b) and Polhemus (1994, 1996) postulated. We should not make the mistake of believing what upper classes purchase is considered fashion and the rest not fashion. Although I do not deny the power of the wearer to convert clothing into fashion, it is the institutions that determine and diffuse which clothes become fashion. There is an interconnection between the production and consumption of fashion. Furthermore, none of the early writers had a place for designers' individual creativity, nor did they anticipate the changes in class structure and attitudes toward authority that would prompt some people to reject upper-class images.

There is a deficiency in the scholarly literature on fashion designers in all social science disciplines. Crane is one of few sociologists who specifically focuses on a discussion on design as an occupation (1993, 1997a, 1997b). Designers are rarely included in the sociological analysis of artists, such as painters, sculptors, writers, dancers, musicians or writers. Crane analyzes the social position of designers in the US, France, the UK and Japan, and also examines the styles that the designers create. She (2000) argues that a single fashion genre, Haute Couture, has been replaced by three major categories of styles, each with its own genres: luxury fashion design, industrial fashion, and street styles. On the other hand, I focus on designers rather than designs (Kawamura 2004), and designers are classified according to different types within the system of hierarchy, and each group of designers constitutes a class, that is the designers who belong to the fashion system and those who do not.

Like Crane, Bourdieu (1980) insists on the importance of the producers of cultural goods. In the case of fashion, it is the fashion designers. These producers can be totally involved and absorbed in their struggles with other producers. They are very much responsible for creating, diffusing and legitimizing clothing as fashion. As barriers between the classes have diminished, there has been a need for someone else to create fashion. The social positions of fashion designers have risen. People have needed someone to follow. With the disappearance of clear class boundaries and the loss of a subject to imitate, the emphasis has shifted from the wearer of fashion to the producer/creator of fashion.

Crane (2000) examines how the nature of fashion organizations affects what is available to consumers, how certain types of consumers influence what is defined as fashion and how the organizations affect designers. The hierarchical structure that was the result of the French fashion trade organization, which is at the core of the system, must be included in the discussion of design as an occupation. Crane argues that by the late 1960s the increasing decentralization and complexity of the fashion system necessitated the development of fashion forecasting, and fashion bureaus play a major role in predicting future trends and what types of clothing will sell. My empirical findings (Kawamura 2004) also show that many of the forecasters make every effort to get into invitation-only fashion shows and predict what may become the future trends. Company designers and retailers from the US and other countries come to Paris to purchase fashion items as samples so as to 'steal' ideas.

The fashion-ological analysis of designers is social organizational and not aesthetic. Fashion is not defined as something more special and the great works of genius. However, the works of designers are essential because the understanding of the social structure and organization of the fashion system includes designers' role in the system and what they produce. Thus we cannot dismiss designers and their designs, their fabrics and silhouettes, and even the production process of types of clothing must be taken into account in order to understand fashion and clothing fully. It is not an intention of Fashion-ology to define creativity, but one can question the meaning of creativity and its labeling process. Fashion systems transform clothing into fashion. Fashion is a symbolic production while clothes are a material production. Fashion is a symbol manifested through clothing.

I have shown (Kawamura 2004) the connection between social institutions of fashion and the legitimation of designers by those institutions. The French fashion trade organization, the principal focus of my research, has endured for well over a century. That persistence directs our attention to the internal systemic structure of the organization. The history of the organization, which lies in the center of the system, shows the changing nature of its structure. The organization was compelled to take measures in order to maintain the exclusivity of French fashion or to ease some of its regulations to bring new designers into the system so that Paris as the fashion capital would survive. The system and its participants constantly negotiate external social situations.

For instance, the Haute Couture organization first differentiated itself from other custom-made clothes, called Confection, in order to make Haute Couture exclusive. The organization has changed membership criteria to allow younger designers to take part. They have introduced a new kind of Haute Couture called Demi-Couture (half-couture) due to the loss of Haute Couture customers and declining profits. The emergence of Kenzo, the first Japanese designer in Paris to enter the French system, was a result of changes taking place in the system that permitted, encouraged or demanded an infusion of something new, different and exotic. At the same time, the arrival of the avant-garde Japanese designers (Issey Miyake, Yohji Yamamoto and Rei Kawakubo) forced the system to expand its boundary and include them. There is a connection between the structure and the process by which individuals are integrated into it. Designers' inclusion into the system is vital because that inclusion labels their activity and designs as 'creative.' Creativity, I argue, is a legitimation and a labeling process. One is not born creative but one becomes, that is, one is identified as, creative.

Designers, Creativity and Social Structure

Actors in the system have shared values to achieve their specific goals. Each participant has individual goals that are met by participation in the system, plays a specific part in the overall system and gets benefits from that participation. The making of designers is not a responsibility of one individual but of a collective activity. One can look at fashion organizations and the fashion system in relation to the people whose collective actions construct the fashion system because there is always a correlation between social structures and the actions of people working collectively. These cooperative networks make fashion happen. All parts, each with specific latent and manifest functions within the institution, are interdependent. None of them is indispensable in the production of fashion. Thus institutions and creators belong to the system that contributed in making Paris the fashion capital. A small number of people in any organization can hold authority. The elites who are in control generally share a common culture, and they mobilize formally and informally in the sense that they act together to defend their position, and use it to their own individual as well as institutional advantage. It is they who act as gatekeepers and construct the legitimate standard of aesthetics of appearance by taking advantage of Paris as their symbolic capital.

While talents and creativity alone are invoked to explain the success and the fame of a fashion designer, understanding the structure of the fashion system is essential to gaining the official designer status. The concept of creativity in fashion is elusive as for any artistic activity, but it is generally, and correctly, assumed that the making of fashion requires special skills. The majority of fashion professionals who have the authority to name creative designers point to their innovativeness and innate talent. Although it is not inaccurate to say that these designers are gifted, these gifts alone do not give the status that the world acknowledges. Every individual has an urge to create something and possesses the seed for creativity, but external forces are required to legitimate that act or the end product as 'creative.' The conception of creativity needs to be questioned. Examining the institutional factors in the social process of the making of a designer will provide some answers to this vexed question.

I am in opposition to the conventional notion that any great art will eventually be recognized because great creators with exceptional talents produce art works with universal aesthetic qualities that are part of universal human cultural values. This theory does not take into consideration the social processes and environment in which creators take part. Since 1970 Japanese designers have enjoyed high reputations in Paris, and no history of fashion in Paris is complete without them. As indicated in my empirical research (Kawamura 2004), it was not only their creativity that made them famous and sent them to Paris. If designers' talent can directly correlate with the prestige and success, these designers could have remained in Japan; wherever they were, according to the conventional view, they would have been discovered by fashion legitimators. Paris is the ultimate 'symbolic capital' (Bourdieu 1984) for designers, for non-Western designers in particular, because 'fashion' is believed to be originally a Western concept. Having been acknowledged by the French fashion system, they have the ticket to go anywhere in the world, and their reputations are guaranteed. The younger Japanese designers are following the same path, and one needs to investigate how they take advantage of the French system and how French recognition has influenced their status in their homeland, Japan.

Thus, by examining in analytical and descriptive detail an institutional realm of fashion about which there is little systematic information, I dismiss the mythical conception of a designer as a 'creative genius' disconnected from social conditions. The institutional structure that surrounds the phenomenon of fashion has been neglected in the studies of fashion. An analysis of designers, especially the Japanese avant-garde designers, can provide the criteria that fashion gatekeepers use in the evaluation of innovative designers. Well-known designers are supposedly creative and have exceptional skills. However, it is the admission into the system that defines designers' creativity. The organizational structure of the system at the time when designers seek to enter the system is crucial. Rei Kawakubo, one of the Japanese avant-garde designers, can be referred to as an example because she uses unique methods to materialize her abstract concepts into actual material clothing. The material fabrication is not the major consideration in defining creativity. The system needs to name creative designers because without them, the system loses the meaning of its existence. The concept of newness must be integrated into the discussion of creativity as these two are the opposite sides of the same coin. What has been previously observed by fashion gatekeepers is never considered new, therefore not creative. We must question, then, new to whom?

Wolff (1993) treats the notion of creativity as the central theme in her book approaching the arts from a traditional notion of 'the artist' or 'the author,' whose creative autonomy is reduced to a series of social, economic and ideological co-ordinates. I use Wolff's analytical framework to understand the link between structure and creativity which appears to be in opposition but are mutually dependent. Creativity is not given and not universal, but produced within a social system (Wolff 1993). Designers express whatever they have internalized using fabrics that are in turn materialized into clothing, but I argue that this has nothing to do with the definition of creativity because it is the system that defines creativity.

The conception of the artist as an unique and gifted individual is a historically specific one, and it dates from the rise of the merchant classes in Italy and France, and from the rise of humanist ideas in philosophy and religious thought (Wolff 1993). It is often believed that the artist is an isolated individual detached from any social institutions. Likewise, designers are known to be gifted and talented by nature. It is frequently believed that the fashion leader has the personality of an artist, an artist of clothes, and like all artists, his or her ability is inborn; the feeling for clothes cannot be taught, either a person possesses the flare or they are without it (Brenninkmeyer 1963: 60). Fashion-ology challenges such a view of the designer.

By participating in the fashion system, designers first earn legal–rational[1] authority, and they are expected to abide by the system's rules and regulations. The fashion system accords charismatic authority, that is the mythic status of 'great designer.' This is a reversal of Weber's (1947) theory of authority in which charismatic authority precedes legal–rational authority. Similarly, the authority of the system arises out of the authority of designers. Charismatic authority rests on a leader's personal qualities, so that the governed submit because of their belief in the extraordinary quality of the specific person, and the legitimacy of charismatic rule thus rests upon the belief in magical powers, revelations, and hero worship (Gerth and Mills 1970). Thus charismatic authority does not require scientific or factual evidence to prove seemingly supernatural talent. It needs instead elements that attract followers to maintain charisma which subsequently creates a hierarchy of those who have that exceptional skills and those who do not. The stratification system is the result of status competition. The charismatic authority of the 'great' designer is ratified, indeed produced, by the fashion system.

Legitimation of the Designer's Creativity

It is often taken as given that the designer must have completely mastered the technical side of dressmaking and have an innate feeling for color harmonies, the balance and arrangement of parts, the matching of different or similar materials and a feeling for rhythm (Brenninkmeyer 1963: 60). However, when one studies to what extent the designer is involved in the actual manufacturing and designing process of a garment, the degree of involvement varies from designer to designer, from company to company. Then the job description of the designer becomes questionable, and then the meaning of creativity also becomes questionable.

What do designers do? They design clothes. Does that mean they only sketch and draw? If so, what is the difference between a designer and a fashion illustrator? Paul Poiret, who was one of the greatest designers and couturiers of the twentieth century, had a fashion illustrator sketch his designs. Then what was his job? He draped, which means he had the skill and knew about garment constructions. Then does this job description apply to all designers? Rei Kawakubo is known for not having had any fashion training (Sudjic 1990), nor had Coco Chanel (Tobin 1994), but they are two of the greatest designers in the history of fashion. There is no specific job description for a designer. Then how are they evaluated? Based on what skills? Zolberg poses a question succinctly:

Inherent in the controversies concerning the nature of art, whether in the art world per se or in the generally problematic cohabitation of sociology and art, is the agency by which it is created, centering on the person- or personage- or the artist. Does it matter who creates the work? How the creator comes to be an artist? Whether the artist works alone or as part of a group? (1990: 107)

The dressmakers/designers used to be judged by the way they created their silhouettes. Madeleine Vionnet, who was apprenticed at the age of eleven to a dressmaker, gradually worked her way up, until she opened her own couture house in 1912 (Steele 1988: 118). It was she who invented the biased cut. Alix Grès, known as Madame Grès, also invented intricate pleating techniques that could not be readily reproduced by anyone else but her. In today's fashion, the focus is less on the actual clothing or its manufacturing process, but rather, on the designer who can produce and reproduce a glamorous, attractive image to the consumers. For example, Issey Miyake, a Japanese designer in Paris who is known for his new and innovative fabrics, works with a creative textile designer, Makiko Minagawa, who comes up with something concrete while Miyake gives out an abstract concept.

The irony is that the designers whose dressmaking and tailoring techniques were exclusive and superb did not survive as an enterprise since the industry gradually shifted its attention towards image-making. Although Chanel did not know much about clothing production, her name continues till this day while the names of Vionnet and Madame Grès remain only in the history of fashion and have disappeared from the commercial market. The star quality is more significant than the skills that the designers possess.

Today, television, radio, newspapers, magazines and movies are often credited with legitimizing fashion change, even with 'creating' fashion since they give intensive and selective exposure to some proposed fashions and ignore others. Their primary role within the present-day fashion system may be that of speeding up fashion change because they show new fashions that are being worn by persons or groups who have the prestige to be legitimitators.

The Star System of Designers

According to Arnold Hauser (1968), the social organization of artistic production changed during the Renaissance and the conception of artist as a genius, and the idea that the work of art is the creation of an autocratic personality. The designer is a relatively modern figure. The social prestige and the nature of occupation change over time. The history of designers shows us that until the mid-nineteenth century those who made clothes did not have much social prestige, and their names were never publicly exposed. After Worth, dressmakers and tailors became the couturiers and designers. They dictated the trends and the tastes which used to originate from court society. Today, designers create images. They have celebrity status and not only control public taste but also create their own image carefully. The very first concept of a designer emerged in France when fashion was institutionalized by the French trade organization. Before that, those who made clothing were not designers. The roles that fabric merchants, dressmakers and tailors played were very different and were restricted and controlled tightly by the guild system.

One of the earliest significant figures in the history of fashion is probably Rose Bertin who was known as a minister of fashion. Her name often appears in the history of French fashion because she helped design clothes with Queen Marie-Antoinette. Bertin was in the world of fashion before Worth and, strictly speaking, she was not a couturière but a *marchande de mode* (De Marly 1980a: 11) who sold bonnets, fans, frills and lace in addition to making clothes. She did not create nor initiate 'fashion.' She was not the producer of fashion. De Marly explains:

> Rose Bertin did not create . . . fashions single-handed: rather they were the outcome of discussions between the queen and her ladies and were then realized by Bertin as actual items of wear. Thus Rose Bertin does not qualify for the title of fashion dictator in the sense of being a completely independent operator who launches new lines at her own establishment, regardless of the opinions of her customers. (1980a: 11)

Dressmakers and tailors merely carried out the ideas devised for them by artists.

The institutionalization of fashion in France from 1868 elevated the status of those who were involved in clothes-making from a craftsperson to designer. Worth was the very first designer whose name was exposed to the public. He was no longer a servant catering to rich women. He was so popular that all women wanted to be dressed by Worth. He changed the whole social organization of dressmaking and the relationship between a couturier and a client. He was authoritative and autocratic and considered himself an artist rather than a dressmaker or a tailor who served the rich. He was the first star designer in history. This technique and methodology prove to be still effective, and probably even more so today as fashion is less about clothing production and more about image production. Many now believe that the role of the fashion leader is skillfully to design models for the select group of rich women who will later be imitated by other groups in the long hierarchy of fashion diffusion, to be a symbol of the modern manner of appearance, to make the fashion of the moment seem so attractive and desirable. In Worth's time the designer or couturier was responsible for designing the creations, and then the design would be handed over to a workroom to be made up as the toile, a trial dress in cheap fabrics like calico or linen, to see how well the design worked, and what problems it might create over construction (De Marly 1990: 12). Such requirements for the designer began to change at the turn of the twentieth century.

Stars in Culture Industries

The star needs to be a single individual. Success in culture production, including fashion, is often the result of the efforts of a combination of insider personnel. Cultural industries have a great deal of appetite for new creative products. The economic and social value declines once the novelty wears off. Stars elevate particular products and help create an identity for an entire network or other culture-producing organization, and this is how stars in cultural industries become brand names. Particular creative artists have risen to star status based on audience reaction. In order to induce demand, culture industries attempt to define stars for the public through advertising. Publicists attempt to create a unique identity for the artist, often woven out of both real and manufactured elements. In the fashion industry, the identity of stars is particularly important. This is because designers personify the clothes they design. The designers and their clothes are intended to portray a certain lifestyle, a way of approaching life or worldview that fans identify with and aspire to.

According to Ryan and Wentworth (1999), the cultural industry has main strategies for bringing the consumer and the product together, such as 1) the development of a classification system of cultural products or 'genres' which provide the distinct content, and 2) the star system which injects personality into mass consumption and allows consumers to form what are sometimes deep emotional attachments. The star system exists not only in fashion but also in the art, book, restaurant, film and music industries among many others. Genre and the star system are attempts to produce something analogous to brand names in cultural industries. Stars cannot be created overnight and, therefore, they make an attempt to cement their visual image by exhibiting original attractive characteristics in many ways. Stars are indispensable because it is part of the ideology of creativity that creative works must have an identifiable author. Creators have their names linked to their creative product and the audience expects to know who the maker of the product is, who the creators are, who the singer and the songwriter are, and who painted the painting. Creative production has not dissolved into the anonymity of industrial production.

The Star Designers since the Turn of the Twentieth Century

How much designers are involved in clothing production is not relevant to consumers, but designers have to be labeled by legitimators as the stars who create fashion. Stars are socially constructed with followers and fans who are bonded to them. In today's world of fashion, designers must become the stars. If not, they remain mere company designers who produce clothing and fashion that are reachable to the masses who want to believe that they have a part in wearing fashionable clothing. The star quality of the designer is not inborn or of nature but is a social construction. The stars are necessary to rejuvenate and revamp the industry. Hollander remarks:

> 'Fashion' is what appears by that name in the media and in designers' collections in shops, after first appearing on runways; and just as in all of show business, it is now connected with famous names and their famous characteristic associations. The stars of 'Fashion' arrive, thrive and fade, new postures and themes flourish until dimmed or swamped by others, all in the context of vast and thrilling corporate risk. (1994: 10–11)

Similarly, Lipovetsky defines the designers' star system as follows:

> the enchanted fabrication of images of seduction ... Like fashion, stars are artificial constructions, and if fashion is the aestheticization of clothing, the star system is the aestheticization of actor – not only their faces but their entire individuality ... .the star system is based on the same values as fashion, on the sacralization of individuality and appearances. Just as fashion is the apparent personalization of ordinary human beings, so the star is the personalization of the actor; just as fashion is the sophisticated staging of the human body, so the star is the media staging of a personality. (1994: 182)

Fashion as an intangible cultural symbol becomes tangible and concrete through the process of personification. Luxurious lifestyles with gala evenings and expensive dresses are associated with fashion. Paul Poiret (1879–1944) was probably a pioneer in publicity and communication. He became as famous as or more famous than the clients he designed for. Although Poiret's couture house does not exist today, unlike Christian Dior or Coco Chanel, Poiret left a number of legacies in the world of fashion. He first apprenticed at Jacques Doucet, a famous couturier at the time, and later at Worth. Then he set up his own couture house. Poiret introduced an empire style,[2] and for that the constriction in the middle of a corset had to be removed. He introduced high waist, slim figures and narrow dresses with very little decoration. His style was criticized as 'lowering the tone of couture' and 'barbaric' (De Marly 1987: 84). His life was very flamboyant, and he organized fancy dress parties and fashion shows with all the publicity he could receive. In 1910, Poiret took the slim style to extreme and created the hobble skirt, a garment so narrow that walking was almost impossible. This created uproar, and criticism poured in from all directions. What was positive about this trend was that it provoked a great deal of sensation, including papal condemnation from Rome (De Marly 1987: 90), which was considered good publicity. Poiret also tried to launch trousers for women. Women were starting to wear bloomers for cycling, but trousers for women as fashionable dress were unheard of. After the First World War, he could not adjust to the change in society and people's taste.

Gabriel Coco Chanel (1883–1971) is one of the greatest and the most famous female star designers in the history of twentieth-century fashion. She was provocative and promiscuous. Like Poiret, her lifestyle was way out of the norm but in different ways. The popular image of Chanel is of a unique genius who created her personal style in isolation from the work of other fashion designers (Tobin 1994). Her biography is just as or more interesting than the styles she innovated, such as jersey sportswear with short skirts. In the belle époque,[3] it was almost a cliché for a man to set up his mistress in the hat business, so that she would be financially independent when he tired of her (Steele 1992: 119). Chanel once said 'I was able to open a high fashion shop, because two gentlemen were outbidding each other for my hot little body' (quoted in Steele 1992: 119). In the early years of her career, Chanel knew little about the technical aspects of dressmaking and was very much dependent on her seamstresses and tailors, but as Steele explains, Chanel's strengths lay elsewhere: in concept and image:

> Her *image* as a modern woman has strongly influenced our perception of her contribution to fashion ... She was a fashion personality. She epitomized the liberated and independent woman ... Chanel ... was the woman that other women wanted to look like. In this sense, she represented the new type of fashion designer, who combined in her person the hitherto masculine role of the fashion 'genius' with the feminine role of fashion leader (not the dressmaker, but the celebrity). Vionnet always denied that a clever man like Poiret or a stylish woman like Chanel could ever equal professional dressmakers like the Callot sisters, and in technical terms this was probably true. But in terms of mass popularity, it was irrelevant. (1992: 120–3)

The image that Chanel was portraying was very different from that of Dior, and he was one of the reasons that Chanel decided to come out of retirement. To her, he was the epitome of the bad, male designer who imposed all sorts of artificial shapes upon women without ever referring to the fundamental nature of women's bodies, and Dior assumed the right to instruct women in remodelling themselves to suit his fantasies; he loved flowers, so let all women bloom into roses. The picutre may be charming, but it does not hold up very well in the real world where the majority of women have to work for a living, and blooming dresses would soon suffer from the blight of travel, weather, children and machines (De Marly 1990: 69).

When ordinary clothes were still rationed, Dior was employing lavish amounts of fabric and the most luxurious and expensive fabrics, such as silk and satin, and that was scandalous. For ordinary women rationing meant that the New Look was impossible to achieve and it was 1948 before the clothing industry could even attempt to copy the style. De Marly explains the image that Dior was creating and supporting:

> Time and time again, he wrote that he was trying to make women more alluring, more seductive, more coquettish, so he subscribed only to the old masculine society's view of women, which the Church fully endorsed, that woman could only be Eve, the eternal temptress, who should be judged on her physical assets alone ... He only knew two types of women, the professional glamour girls and entertainers, and the rich. Women professors, doctors, writers, administrators and commandants, did not exist in Dior's world. (1990: 69)

Dior was extremely successful as an enterprise, and by 1954, he had 900 employees, of whom forty-six were on the administrative side, and the rest selling and making clothes. In 1955 the figure was put at 1,000 staff, in twenty-eight workrooms and five buildings. He was the biggest couturier in Paris although still smaller than Worth who had been with a staff of 1,200 (De Marly 1990). Dior's biggest achievement was reviving the couture industry in Paris after the Second World War, bringing foreign clients back from all over the world. After the city had disappeared under the Nazi heel in the summer of 1940, London and New York had become the chief fashion centers so the press was concentrated on them. Dior attracted the international headlines notifying the world that Paris couture was back and alive. The French fashion industry wanted to create a star, and for that Dior was selected.

He died of a heart attack in 1957. Then Yves Saint Laurent was appointed to design for the house. His first show was in 1958, and his last was in 1960. Then Marc Bohan was summoned from the London branch. He had joined Piguet's in 1945, spent a couple of years with Molyneux, and then gone to Patou in 1950 from where Dior recruited him. Bohan was at Dior until 1989.

A network of star designers reproduced another group or generation of star designers.[4] For instance, Balmain was trained by Molyneux who began his career with Lucile; Givenchy worked for Fath, Piguet, Lelong and Schiaparelli before launching out on his own; Griffe worked for Vionnet who started at Doucet. Christian Dior (1905–1957) sold his design to couture houses, to Patou, Schiaparelli, Nina Ricci, Maggy Pouf, Piguet, Molyneux, Worth, Paquin and Balenciago among others. He knew nothing about the construction of clothes, so the designer Georges Geoffrey introduced Dior to the couturier Robert Piguet who trained him as a designer in 1938. He had crossed the threshold into Haute Couture. In 1941, Dior received an invitation to join Lucien Lelong's couture house back in Paris to work alongside Pierre Balmain, who opened his store in 1944 and had trained under Molyneux between 1934 and 39. Dior was very much influenced by Worth and Molyneux.

Hierarchy among Designers in the Fashion System

The designers are most stratified in the French system of fashion: couturiers who design Haute Couture, designers who design Prêt-à-Porter and company designers who design for the mass-produced apparel companies. This group classification began with the institutionalization of fashion.

A symbolic boundary divides designers in the French fashion system and those outside the system. Those in the system form the dominant position with 'couturiers' in the upper stratum and 'creators' in the lower one. These particular groups of designers can be the main focus of one's research because they are the major players in the game. Fashion ensures the functioning of a system of dominant and subordinate positions within a social order. Fashion is ideological in that it is also part of the process in which particular social groups, in this case elite designers, establish, sustain and reproduce positions of power and relations of dominance and subordination. The positions of dominance and subordination appear natural and legitimate, not only to those in positions of dominance, but also to those in subordinate positions. Fashion and the medium of fashion, that is clothing, offer means to make inequalities of social economic status appear legitimate, and therefore, acceptable. A legitimate reason for excluding those designers who remain outside the system is that they do not have sufficient creativity and talent.

According to Gramsci (1975), hegemony refers to the situation where certain social groups or certain fractions of social groups in positions of dominance exert their social authority as a result of their power appearing and being experienced as legitimate. He argues that the ruling class or group controls not only property but, even more importantly, the means of producing beliefs about reality. Accordingly, French hegemony over fashion is treated as given and unquestionable. However, I argue that fashion professionals and institutions in the system deliberately make efforts to sustain the structure and hegemony. Hegemony is a moving battle that must be constantly negotiated, re-fought and re-won on a series of battlefields (Gramsci 1975). The designers within the system which has the hegemonic structure grant themselves privilege and status to distance themselves from other designers who are engaging in the same activities and tasks but do not have the equivalent social and symbolic capital. The boundary between different groups of designers corresponds to the public who consumes respective clothing styles.

The institutionalization of fashion in France resulted in the demarcation between two groups of designers, just as it drew a line between those who consumed the latest fashion and those who imitated what the other class wore (Simmel 1957[1904]; Veblen 1957[1899]). The designers in the system, whom I call 'elite designers,' reaffirm their status through continuous participation in the regular fashion shows which serve as a ritual that reproduces and reinforces the symbolic meaning of fashion, much like the Durkheimian analysis of religion (Durkheim 1965[1912]). However, this demarcation is also democratic, arbitrary and fluid not only for consumers but also for designers. With institutionalization, fashion, once reserved for the elites, has become more democratized and accessible to the masses. Institutional innovation has had an effect on the legitimation of new designers and new styles. It institutionalized elite clothes as Haute Couture (high fashion or high sewing) and Prêt-à-Porter (ready-to-wear). Recently a new category, Demi-Couture (half-couture), was added, although still not officially institutionalized, in an attempt to nurture and welcome younger designers to the couture group.

Fashion-ology denies the romantic notion of the designer as genius, removed from the usual condition of ordinary people by virtue of the gift of artistic/creative genius. It moves away from the idea of artist-as-creator. It treats designers as one of the participants in social relations of fashion. As Steele (1988: 9) points out:

The fashion leadership of Paris was not due to any particular spirit of frivolity or progressiveness on the part of Parisians. Nor is Paris fashion the product of individual creative genius, although this concept continues to play a large part in the mythology of fashion. The many anecdotes about the 'dictatorship' or the 'genius' of Paris fashion designers indicate a profound misunderstanding of the fashion process.

We should not overemphasize the individual artist as unique creator of a work because to do so writes out of the account the numerous other people involved in the production of any work, and also draws attention away from the various socially constituting and determining processes involved. As Wolff explains (1993: 134), the traditional concept of the artist as creator depends on an unexamined view of the subject and conceives of a person with no institutional ties, but in fact the artist is constituted in social and cultural processes. Similarly, Becker (1982) asserts that the individual artist is transformed into a team player, one of many collaborators. As he presents the process of artistic production, there is little difference between creation and reception.

Our attention is directed to the social process of creating a designer, to how people become designers, to how and what they make and create, and to how they remain as known designers and maintain their positions. We are not concerned with the manufacturing, pattern-making or draping processes that are taken to create an item of clothing, although these are interesting area to focus on since every designer uses a slightly different technique and methodologies in the manufacturing process.

Conclusion

Designers need to be legitimated to be successful and, therefore, they must be a member of the system or participate in it. For that, they need to come to one of the fashion cities where the system is in place. There is a view shared by many that creators of artwork, including fashion designers, have inborn, talent that cannot be easily reproduced or copied by others. The fashion-ological perspective of these designers, although they are important in the production of fashion, are part of the collective production of fashion in which large numbers of people participate.

5

Production, Gatekeeping and Diffusion of Fashion

The fashion system creates symbolic boundaries between what is fashion and what is not fashion and also determines what the legitimate aesthetic taste is. Producers of fashion, including designers and other fashion professionals who are agents of fashion, make a contribution in defining a taste that is represented as items of fashionable clothing. After clothes are manufactured, they go through the transformation process and the mechanism of fashion production passing through different institutions. Individuals involved in the production of clothing manufacture items of garments, and then those items must go through the legitmation process and pass the criteria set by gatekeepers[1] of fashion before they are disseminated to the public. As noted in Chapter 4, designers are involved in both clothing as well as fashion production processes, and without the designers, there would be no fashion to start with. However, the designers alone cannot produce fashion, nor can they sustain the fashion system that leads to the making of fashion culture. Other producers of fashion besides designers, such as advertisers and marketers, also make a major contribution in fashion culture. Fashion is about change and the illusion of novelty. Those who take part in the production of fashion help create the ideology of fashion and determine which items of clothing will be defined as fashion and fashionable.

The link between the production/distribution of clothing and the dissemination of the idea of fashion is interdependent. The apparel industries serve as the primary traffic-builders and producers of profitable sales for, first of all, the customers of the textile industries and are, in turn, dependent on the retailers for the purchase and distribution of the goods they manufacture. The fashion system has two types of diffusion agents: 1) designers who take part in seasonal fashion shows in Paris, London, Milan and New York, and are frequently the very conspicuous individuals who establish themselves as arbiters of good taste and surround themselves with a cult of personality, and 2) fashion journalists, editors, advertisers,

73

marketers/merchandisers and publicists. We must find out the actual agencies through which fashion works so that we can review concrete ways in which fashion is formed and felt.

This chapter explores diffusion theories of fashion from individual and institutional perspectives, aesthetic judgments of fashion, diffusion strategies, such as fashion dolls in the past and fashion shows today, fashion propaganda through the use of advertising, and technological influences on fashion diffusion.

Diffusion Theories of Fashion

Diffusion theories of fashion seek to explain how fashion is spread through interpersonal communication and institutional networks, and they assume that the fashion phenomenon is not ambiguous nor unpredictable. As Horn and Gurel explain:

> When clothing behavior is expressed in fashion, the behavior is still regular and predictable. Fashions in any area of life, especially fashions in clothing, are not random and purposeless. They reflect the cultural patterns of the times. Fashions follow a progressive and irreversible path from inception through acceptance to culmination and eventual decline, and they also tend to parallel to some extent the larger events of history. (1975: 2)

Diffusion is the spread of fashion within and across social systems. Whereas the adoption process focuses on individual decision-making, the diffusion process centers on the decision of many people to adopt an innovation. How fast and how far an innovation diffuses are influenced by several factors: formal communications from the mass media, personal communications among current adopters and potential adopters, the persuasive influence of consumer leaders and other agents, and the degree to which the innovation is communicated and transferred from one social system to another. It is often believed that it is the designers who impose a new fashion upon the public in order to stimulate the market and the economy. But clothing manufacturers are necessary because they work with fashion producers who produce the idea of fashion. Consumers always want something fashionable and follow fashion because fashion is believed to be desirable.

Diffusion theories of fashion can focus on individuals, which can give a small-scale analysis, and on institutions, which is a systematic, large-scale approach. One can take into account both psychological and sociological elements in the fashion diffusion. Fashion can be studied either from the point of view of the individual as the early psychologists indicated, or from the point of view of the structure and function of society as a whole as many sociologists would do. Fashion adoption and diffusion could also be the result of individual aspirations and necessities as they are formed by the social system with which the individual comes into contact.

Influential Leaders of Fashion Diffusion

In the context of clothing fashion adoption, innovativeness and opinion leadership are highly related. Moreover, in societies oriented toward change, the overlap of innovation and opinion leadership is greater than in more tradition-oriented cultures. Diffusion theories of fashion seek to explain how fashion is adopted by many people within a social system. A social system might be the residents of a city, the students of a school, a group of friends, or any other group of individuals who regularly interact. Each interaction can be considered an act of communication through which information and influence concerning an innovation, such as new styles of clothing, can be spread.

According to Katz and Lazarsfeld (1955), informal person-to-person communication influences everyday situations, and their study showed that verbal personal influence was the most effective type of communication in fashion situations. It was the reaction of friends and acquaintances or salespeople on seeing a woman's hairdo or dress that counted, and in most cases, women influence other women like themselves. Approval and admiration will encourage behavior of the same kind; disapproval or disdain will tend to bring about a change in dress. In this way, fashion diffusion can first be explained from a micro-scale interpersonal perspective. Communications can also enter a social system from other social systems. Ultimately, awareness of the innovation is diffused to most members of the social system through the combined influence of external sources and interpersonal communications within the system. Then the innovation is recognized as fashion, and for that, legitimation is indispensable.

Legitimizing newly introduced forms of elements of dress as fashion is a step required for their acceptance. Various mechanisms for legitimizing fashion change have prevailed at different times in the history of fashionable dress. One has been the use of fashionable forms of dress by well-known high-prestige figures, whose stamp of approval signals to those of lesser social visibility or eminence that a new fashion is acceptable and desirable. The influential leaders of fashion diffusion have ranged from politically powerful kings, such as Louis XIV, to those associated with such a ruler, for instance Louis XIV's and Louis XV's mistresses, including Madame de Montespan, Madame de Maintenan, Madame de Pompadour and Madame du Barry, to celebrities, such as actors, actresses and singers.

The fashion system invents new cultural meanings, and this invention is undertaken by opinion leaders who help shape and refine existing cultural meaning, encouraging the reform of cultural categories and principles. These groups and individuals are sources of meaning for the masses, and they invent and deliver symbolic meanings that are largely constructed by prevailing cultural co-ordinates established by cultural categories and cultural principles. These groups are also permeable to cultural innovations, changes in style, value and attitudes which they then pass along to the subordinate parties who imitate them (McCracken 1988: 80). Therefore, in order to understand the diffusion of fashion, we must first consider the roles played by those social groups most directly connected with its propagation. It does not matter who plays the roles, but it is very important that the roles are played.

In the aristocratic society of seventeenth- and eighteenth-century Europe, the fashion leaders were members of royalty. Their showcases were the royal courts. The best artisans were called upon to adorn the sumptuously elegant costumes that were paraded in the splendid setting of the French court. As patrons of the theater, royal families donated their clothes to their favorite actors, making the theater a vehicle for popularizing the fashions set by the royal court (Brenninkmeyer 1963). This policy continued in France until the Revolution, when actresses began creating their own costumes for the stage. Then a period of deterioration followed, and it was not until the years 1875 to 1918 that the theater again became the center for fashion inspiration. Fashions began to emerge from stage costumes and hairstyles often acquired the name of the actress who wore them.

In democratic societies where there are no royals, politicans' wives, such as Jackie Kennedy, and celebrities, like Madonna, have become the leaders of fashion. The works of the designers receive attention when the designs are worn by celebrities and photographers. In this way, producers of fashion and consumers of fashion complement each other in maintaining the ideology of fashion.

Fashion cannot be entirely accounted for in terms of individuals, either on the side of the producers or the wearers. For a new style to become fashionable, it must in some way appeal to a large number of people. The clothing habits of an individual are the result of group life.

Institutional Diffusion

In the 1960s and 1970s, when much of the work on fashion using diffusion models was done, diffusion models were conceptualized as relatively unorganized interpersonal processes, but today, fashion diffusion is highly organized and managed within cultural production systems that are intended to maximize the extent of diffusion (Crane 1999: 15). Similarly, according to Sorokin, diffusion is not limited to voluntary imitation: 'Some values are imposed, some others penetrate before a population even has an idea of these values ... [they] want them because they have come in contact with them or because they have been imposed ... Therefore, one cannot claim that in penetration of the values, the inner desire to have them precedes the outer acceptance of them' (1941: 634).

Fashion-ologiy looks at the macro institutional and micro personal diffusion methods. People diffuse specific items of clothing as fashionable because they believe that they are fashionable. Therefore, we must investigate how the consumers come to know them as the fashionable items of the time. However, large-scale diffusion processes such as those affecting fashionable clothing are difficult to study systematically (Crane 1999: 13), and so what Fashion-ology can provide is individuals and institutions involved in the diffusion process of fashion, and it does not try to discover exactly how long items of garments take to be labeled as fashion and remain fashionable. Changes in the relationships between fashion organizations and their publics have affected what is diffused, how it is diffused, and to whom.

The source of fashion diffusion used to be a highly centralized system, initially started in Paris. Innovators belonged to a community that could be understood in terms of Becker's concept of art world, a cluster of individuals and organizations involved in the production, evaluation, and dissemination of a specific form of culture (1982). Fashion worlds comprised designers, publicists, owners of trendy fashion boutiques and local fashion publics, consisting of fashion-conscious individuals. Opinion leaders included editors of leading fashion magazines and highly visible fashion consumers, such as society women, movie stars, and popular music stars (Crane 1999: 16). Awareness of fashion innovations was stimulated by fashion printed in fashion magazines and periodicals.

There is a view that the centralized fashion system has been replaced by another system, and according to Crane (1999) fashion designers in several countries create designs for small publics in global markets. Trends are now set by fashion forecasters, fashion editors, and department store buyers. Industrial manufacturers are consumer driven, and market trends originate in many types of social groups, including adolescent urban subcultures, and consequently, fashion emanates from many sources and diffuses in various ways to different publics (Crane 1999: 13). At the same time, the distinction between production and consumption is becoming increasingly hazy and blurry. The diffusion of fashion has become more difficult to study because the creation of fashion has become less centralized. The increasing decentralization and complexity of the fashion system has necessitated the development of fashion forecasting, which began in 1969. Forecasters consult with fabric designers to predict colors and fabrics a few years before a particular style is marketed.

Sociological Theories of Fashion Diffusion

Diffusion studies point out that they are addressing the spread of an item, idea, or practice over time to adopting individuals, groups, or corporate units that are embedded in channels of communication, social structures, such as networks, communities or classes, and social values or culture (Katz, Levin and Hamilton 1963: 147).

Sociological theories of fashion diffusion emerge out of the classical discourse discussed in Chapter 2. Two sociological models of diffusion have generally been applied to fashion. First, the classical model of the diffusion of fashion, exemplified by Simmel's theory that new styles are first adopted by upper-class elites and then the working class. The social processes underlying this model are imitation, social contagion, and differentiation (McCracken 1985). Tarde (1903) did an empirical study of public opinion and mass communication and made diffusion central to his thinking. He used the concept of imitation as the basis for his general theory and especially for his theory of diffusion. He talks about the direction of flow, typically from superior to inferior, which has been called trickle-down and also explains the general proposition that the diffusion of ideas precedes their material expression. He insists that desires precede the means of their satisfaction and that belief precedes ritual which is a collective action.

Second, the alternative to this top-down model is a bottom-up model in which new styles emerge in lower-status groups and are later adopted by higher-status groups. Both models assume widespread adoption of a particular fashion and a process of 'social saturation' in which the style or fad eventually becomes overused (Sproles 1985). In the second model, the innovators generally emerge from communities in urban areas that are seedbeds for other types of innovation, such as popular music and the arts. To be disseminated to a larger audience, innovations have to be discovered and promoted. According to Crane (1999: 16), innovators tend to be small firms that are created by individuals who belong to the communities in which the innovations originate. If the style or fad shows signs of becoming popular, large firms begin to produce their versions of it and to market it aggressively.

Gatekeepers: Making Aesthetic Judgments

Articles about fashion are featured regularly in most national and local newspapers, a well as in magazines for women. Despite its high profile in the media, fashion is not generally regarded as a topic serious enough to appear on the 'real news' pages. Fashion is a luxury and is considered trivial, frivolous and fun. As discussed in Chapter 1, this accounts for the way fashion is treated as a woman's topic – even men's fashions appear on women's pages of newspapers and in women's magazines, and it is assumed that women are interested in fashion in a way that most men are not (Rouse 1989). However, fashion writings in the print media have important functions for fashion diffusion. In order for designers to be known and become world famous, they need to be legitimated by those who have the power and authority to influence, such as editors from major fashion magazines. Recognition by them gives the designers the prestige and confirmation that they are talented.

Fresh ideas in fashion design or any field of creative endeavor are news, and new styles attract attention, especially in a culture where people tend to believe that everything new is admirable. The creative couture designer and his or her high fashion models are widely reported in the mass media which confers status. A rise in the social standing of individuals and/or things commands favorable attention in print or on the air. Every fashion periodical, whether it caters to the fashion professionals, the high fashion world, women in general or the younger population, enjoys the trust of and acceptance by a large portion of the audience it serves. The items it reports are accepted as 'superior' pieces and the magazine is considered an important source of information to its readers.

Fashion is the grand motor force of taste (Bell 1976[1947]: 89), and the influence of fashion goes beyond individual taste and our past perceptions of fashion; it molds our concept of what is beautiful. In his analysis of taste and social structure, Bourdieu (1984) presents both an empirical study of consumer habits and an interpretive theory that sees in clothing or fashion a communication and representation of more general orientations to lifestyles. In his surveys of the French population, he found sharp differences in both clothing worn and the nature of clothing/fashion among various classes and occupational groups. Aesthetics and beauty are not important for the blue-collar working class as they focus on the functionality. Among the bourgeoisie, the opposite is the case. Clothing is a way to express their aesthetic taste. They are preoccupied with considerations of aesthetic consequences. Bourdieu reads the empirical differences as evincing the existence of distinctive class-based tastes, as part of the fundamental and deep-seated styles of life. The bourgeoisie deny the primary, material function of clothing and fashion. The metaphoric attributes are connected by a common vision of the world, by a way of stylizing activity. People's taste in clothing and desire to be viewed as fashionable are constructed by institutional factors.

The history of fashion in the West is the history of an ever-changing conception of beauty, an aesthetic which is continually dying and for ever being renewed. Social scientists concerned with aesthetics differ in orientation from scholars more clearly associated with aesthetic or humanist fields (Zolberg 1990: 53). For instance, art historians assume that beauty is inherent, and it is their job to discover absolute beauty. Based on that premise, no one creates fashion, for we are born into a society in which fashion already exists; it exists because it pleases and, because it pleases, our aesthetic affections are predetermined for us (Bell 1976[1947]: 90–1). But for social scientists, beauty is a social construction, and anything can potentially become beautiful and aesthetic, and it depends on the context in which it is placed.

Most participants in the system make aesthetic judgments frequently. The judgments produce reputations for the designers and their works. Thus, the participation becomes crucial. The value of fashion arises from the consensus of the participants in the fashion system, and those participants who control access to distribution channels become influential. People search for fashionable items because they are made to believe that fashion is better and more aesthetic than non-fashion.

Writers and reporters of fashion can be divided into two groups (Kawamura 2004): journalists and editors. Both play a large part in making a style the fashion, for they can interpret a designer's ideas to a public that is not comprised of fashion professionals and give them immense publicity. Their choice is of great significance to designers and buyers alike. The fashion gatekeepers resemble in this respect the gatekeepers in the world of art (Becker 1982) and music (Hirsch 1972). It is their responsibility to observe innovations and decide what is fashion and what is not, or what is ephemeral and what will endure. After they have completed their process of selection and evaluation, they engage in a process of dissemination with which they make their choices known. Journalists and editors are gatekeepers, and they review aesthetic, social and cultural innovations as they first emerge and judge some as important and others as trivial. They, along with consumers, have the power of discovering interesting new designers. Fashion is an important influence on what we wear and what we think. Consumers are informed of fashionable clothes, fashionable shapes of colors, fashionable bodies, fashionable faces and fashionable people.

Above all, fashion magazines have an important function to fulfill because they directly serve the interests of the fashion industry. They diffuse ideas to encourage the selling of latest styles. These magazines appeared prior to and after the First World War and have since profited immensely from the improvements in the techniques of photography and illustration (Brenninkmeyer 1963: 82). The art of fashion photography that began in the 1920s steadily improved over the years and can be used as important visual record. It has, at the same time, accelerated fashion promotion. It has now become one of the most important means of fashion propaganda to be seen in magazines and newspapers.

Fashion Journalists

Fashion journalists write for daily papers whose reports reach a large public. The fashion journalist is usually only a reporter and not a critic. Architects, painters, writers or musicians expect their work to be severely criticized by critics and must brace themselves to receive critical remarks but not the fashion designer. In order to create a mystique, and possibly because fashion is too ephemeral for a standard of comparison to be established, harsh criticism is more often the exception than the rule. This creates a very different climate from the conventional art criticisms and reportage and is largely responsible for the vast amount of descriptive writings about fashion.

One of the most controversial issues in mass media reporting is the conflict between the advertising department and editorial comment. Because the mass media are mainly supported by investments from advertisers rather than from subscribers, it is difficult for the journalists to report fashion news impartially. Designers become the beneficiaries of fashion reporting, which can bring fame and notoriety to their names, and the supplies of advertising money keep the magazines in business. This reciprocal dependency does not encourage unbiased fashion reporting.

Fashion Magazine Editors

Fashion editors write for fashion magazines, where the role of writer merges into the role of merchandiser/stylist. While the journalists' major task is fashion reportage, fashion editors are directly connected to retail stores and indirectly to manufacturers. They together play a major role in producing fashion as an image and maintaining and continuing the belief in fashion. Fashion is portrayed in such a way that it is desirable and highly valued in society. Fashion editors and buyers both from stores and the wholesale trade frequently confer together, for one wants to tell her readers where the new fashions can be found, and the other knows that magazines mold public opinion and can help to sell their goods. This is collaboration between press and trade.

A good fashion editor can be the pivot around which revolves the whole complicated apparatus of launching a new idea, all parts of which must be carefully coordinated if it is to be successful. Once a decision is made to promote a certain line or color, all the selected manufacturers of garments, fabrics and accessories must be approached and agree to cooperate in order to produce the required goods at the right time. The advertising managers of the various firms, in addition to those of the shops who will eventually retail the goods, arrange publicity and possibly take space in the editor's paper; the store buyers agree to carry sufficient goods to back the advertising campaigning, the manufacturers to deliver at a given date, and the stores to devote window displays to the new idea, in which enlargements of the magazine's pages will probably feature. All these phases must coincide with each other and with the date of publication. Thus an editor's selection of just one style from a couture house in Paris may ultimately result in a series of window displays throughout the country, the sale of many thousands of dresses, and the boosting of a new fashion.

The fashion editor, however, has two potent weapons: silence and space. She can ignore collections she considers bad, and she can give the largest possible amount of space to those she thinks are good, with priority in placing and the preference, if any, of color reproductions. Like fashion reporters, few editors can totally ignore advertisers and their demands, for it is on advertising revenue that a fashion paper depends.

Diffusion Strategies from Fashion Dolls to Fashion Shows

Fashion Dolls

At one time new styles were suggested to clients by sketches accompanied with bolts of material or if a complete dress was produced, it was shown on a wooden dummy, not worn by a living woman. Long before life-size models had been thought of, fashion dolls, or milliner's mannequins as they were called, were used to spread the knowledge of new fashions. Fashion dolls were said to be the first means of circulating the latest styles of dress. It became the practice in Paris to display two life-size dolls dressed in the current fashions. 'La Grande Pandora' was fitted out from head to toe each time the fashions changed. The smaller of the dolls, 'La Petite Pandora,' even wore the appropriate underclothes. As early as 1391, Charles VI of France sent the Queen of England full-sized dolls wearing the latest styles made to the Queen's measurements (Diehl 1976: 1).

French fashion dolls[2] became popular in the seventeenth and eighteenth centuries and were sent to all parts of Europe, and as far away as Russia, by milliners, dressmakers and hairdressers. They were considered indispensable to the general export of French fashion novelties. These dolls illustrated current styles in real jewelry as well as hair and dress styles. As France and the French court became politically powerful, the European capitals became very dependent on the flow of dolls from France for fashion news. Rose Bertin, the best known French dressmaker of her day, also used the dolls as advertisements for her services. She outfitted Marie-Antoinette and her model dolls in her creations.

A woman selected a pattern or a style from a fashion doll. She would next select fabric and trimmings, and her final stop would be the dressmaker's shop where the garment was made according to specifications. The popularity of fashion dolls lasted well into the nineteenth century when they were gradually superseded by French fashion plates and, later, fashion magazines (Diehl 1976: 2).

Fashion Shows

What is a fashion show? By definition, a fashion show is a presentation of merchandise on live models. A good show makes one or more general statements about fashion while at the same time showing individual and specific items to support or illustrate these comments. The items must be authoritative, pulled together, edited by the store for the customer (Diehl 1976: 16). Fashion shows as we have today began in France after the institutionalization of fashion.

The living mannequin was the invention of the British couturier in Paris Charles Worth. When he opened his own store in 1858, he not only revolutionalized the couture by designing for an individual woman's type and personality, but he used his wife, Marie, to model his creations in his salon. As he became more successful, he employed a number of mannequins to show his collections to consumers, and those mannequins walked about in the salon or down the runway. By the early 1900s, the use of live models to show fashions to private customers and the press was well established, both inside the couture houses and outside, at special galas and social events (Diehl 1976: 7). By 1911, even in the US, living models were used as a regular part of fashion promotions for retailers as well as manufacturers.

The fashion show owes a great deal of its development to the inventiveness of Worth and to the showmanship of Paul Poiret. While Worth created the modern couture, Poiret extended its range. Poiret radically changed the feminine silhouette and, in the process, developed techniques of fashion promotion that we continue to use. He used his promotional instincts to generate free publicity. He toured chic resorts, Russia and various other countries, making personal appearances and giving fashion showings which were tremendous successes. He was among the first couturiers to parade mannequins at the races, showing pieces from his latest collection to great effect. Throughout his career, he entertained on a lavish scale, throwing huge parties, theatrical presentations and costume balls. They were colorful extravaganzas, well covered in the press (De Marly 1980a).

The House of Paquin also made several contributions to the fashion show. The couturier was more conservative than Poiret, but Paquin began the practice of showing at big social gatherings. He paraded his models at the racetrack and at opening nights at the opera. Paquin also staged a tableau as the finale to his openings – in one show he presented twenty mannequins in white evening dresses. Patou also had an impact on the fashion show in several areas. He introduced gala evenings which were aimed at Paris society and even more strongly at the press.

The Significance of Fashion Shows

The fashion show is a tool of retailing with one basic purpose, that is to sell merchandise. The show must have entertainment value to hold the audience's attention. Another reason for a show might be public relations.

Clothes are sold via a 'merchandising' approach. A fashion is created and promoted to the retailer who stocks it. It is touted in the fashion publications and appears so irresistible that the consumer goes to their favorite store and buys it. The primary thrust in fashionable items is toward the trade. The retailer is critical because the consumer must be able to see, feel and try on the article for a sale to be made in the store they shop at. Conversely, the sale cannot be made if the article is not accessible to the consumer. Clothes are merchandised and marketed as fashion, and they are pushed through the distribution pipeline from manufacturer to retailer to consumer.

The marketing approach requires for the needs of the consumer to be identified specifically and a new product is created to satisfy a need, or an existing product is repositioned or remarketed in line with that need. Advertising to the consumer has concentrated on creating desire for fashion while it is clothing that satisfies the need. Fashion has been the ingredient that sells clothing. Clothing is a basic human need while fashion is not. This is one way to differentiate fashion from clothing. Authoritative fashion statements made by journalists and editors must go beyond the clothing to include accessories and beauty hints included in the broad area covered by the word 'fashion,' and in presenting the fashion story, they must include all the elements of a good, newsworthy story.

Fashion shows have been particularly important for fashion dissemination. A strategy used by French fashion professionals was to centralize fashion in Paris to keep Haute Couture with a Paris label the privilege of an elite. Copies of French styles and designs were the next best thing to Couture. In return for an agreement to purchase toile,[3] paid for in advance as part of the entry ticket, buyers attended the collections and selected designs to put into production. *La Chambre Syndicale de la Couture Parisienne*, a couture trade organization established in 1911, was responsible for timetabling the shows and enforcing strict rules governing publicity and reproduction. Photography and sketching were forbidden. At the cheaper end of the market, mass manufacturers relied on published sources, including the increasing number of fashion forecasting journals. Fashion magazines relayed the highlights of the Paris collections to an international audience (Mendes and de la Haye 1999: 139).

Technological Influences on Fashion Diffusion

It is also important to remember that fashionable clothes became widely available due to technological advances in clothing manufacturing. Fashion was democratized at a fast pace after the invention of sewing and embroidery machines. Worth's big business was helped a great deal by technology. De Marly explains:

Charles Frederick Worth would not have thrived without the technological developments of the day. For instance, the scale of his international dressmaking was only possible throughout the growth of railway, steamship and telegraph systems. Also, Maison Worth could not have turned out hundreds of ball gowns a week, without the improvement in sewing machines to do most of the seams; the finishing, of course, was still by hand. By 1871, he had a staff of 1,200 which was a very different scale of business from the dressmaker with a few dozen seamstresses in her attics. (1980a: 23)

Technological advances started a chain reaction throughout interrelated industries. For instance, sheer wool did not become fashionable until the mechanization of the combing operation made the worsted industry possible. Form-fitting knitted underwear and thin stockings followed the invention of suitable knitting machinery.

The enormous expansion of the women's garment and fashion industries was the result of technical and industrial interrelationships. A shift from production of garments in the home to large-scale production in the factory is dependent upon a ready supply of cloth, which is dependent on the availability of yarn. Lower costs, which increase consumption and enlarge production, are dependent upon the invention of suitable stitching machinery which, in turn, is dependent on the availability on suitable sewing thread, which is dependent on the development of mechanical combs.

Furthermore, modern society resulted in mass production and improved methods of transport, and distribution have made it possible to supply copies of all the newest and exclusive models rapidly, in great numbers, and at relatively low prices, so that women of moderate means in small provincial towns can wear clothes of practically the same design as those that were introduced by the leaders of fashion.

Fashion Propaganda through Advertising

Ideas about fashion are spread through the population by organized means of mass propaganda. One function of fashion propaganda through advertising is to stimulate a desire for the same thing at the same time in a large number of people to build collective belief among consumers. In the technical and industrial age in which we live, the possibilities of influencing masses of people are innumerable. Merton defined propaganda as 'any and all sets of symbols which influence opinion, belief or action on issues regarded by the community as controversial' (1957: 265). Individuals are always on the outlook for what they should have, do or look like, to fit into the appropriate group structure because the majority of modern people no longer live under the influence of ancestral traditions. People in modern society are susceptible to all kinds of propaganda. They read newspapers, current periodicals, advertisements and films to discover what the latest fashion trends are. They wear what other people would like to see them in and thus it becomes important for them to know what is fashionable and what may fit into the framework of social life.

The immediate aim of advertising is to make a product known; in a broader sense it helps to overcome inertia and stimulate people to action.

Advertising works as a potential method of meaning transfer by bringing the consumer good and a representation of the culturally constituted world together within the frame of a particular advertisement. They visualize the fashion belief in a more material sense, and therefore, they must be attractive and desirable so they make consumers want to be fashionable.

According to Millerson (1985: 102), to a greater or lesser extent, all fashion products tend to be aspirational: the product is positioned substantially or slightly above consumer reality toward the kind of person the target group would like to be, and society creates people's desire to purchase and willingness to wear new as opposed to past fashion looks. The consumer is swayed by advertising in areas where it really does not matter. One may switch from one fashion brand to another only because it appears to make a little difference, and one feels that there is a difference.

This is why a great deal of investment goes into national brand advertising. If the consumer can be made brand conscious and brand loyal, even in an unimportant area, it can mean financial success for a company or a designer. The brand name in fashion can stand for the designer, the manufacturer, or the store, and fashion journalists and editors always have news to report simply by showing the latest styles. The purpose of using brands is to build a market. A brand is a device, sign or symbol which is used to identify products so the advertiser can reap the benefits of any demand created. Through a brand name the manufacturer hopes to build prestige for their product, to differentiate it from others in the consumer's mind, and lessen price competition by creating loyal customers who are reluctant to accept other brands. Brand names help consumers repeat a purchase found satisfactory or avoid one that is unsatisfactory. Where fashion companies specialize in one area of design, fashion goods labels become identified with a design style and occasion-type of garment, offering certain quality at a certain price. As long as the designer is consistent with the image that is provided, the brand is a guide for the consumer. The use of brand names is a form of persuasive advertising, a type of propaganda.

Before something can really become a fashion, it must be capable of being labeled. In retrospect, it is clear that there has been a name or phrase attached to most significant changes in fashion. A label is at first only a shorthand method of describing a new style that has been introduced by a designer or a fashion leader. If this style becomes a mass fashion, the label will become known to many people, spread quickly over a wide territory, and become identified with that particular time. A label that wakens a uniform favorable response may be necessary for the general adoption of a style. A sociological study on the effect of symbols on collective behavior has pointed out that a symbol that arouses uniform feelings toward the object is a necessary condition for uniform group action. Many examples of fashion labeling, such as Christian Dior's A-line and H-line, seem to support the belief that it is not possible to launch an idea as fashion unless it can be labeled. 'Fashion' itself is already a label, and thus a dress needs to become 'fashion.' A label, some catchy slogan built around people and events, focuses attention in any campaign. Certainly a name, easy to remember, is a desired feature of any new product fighting for attention in mass media reporting.

Conclusion

The fashion system is about fashion production and not clothing production. Individuals, such as influential leaders of fashion, and institutions that help create and spread fashion, such as fashion magazines and newspaper periodicals, are participants in the system. When we separate clothing production from fashion production, the difference between clothing and fashion become even more succinct. Fashion is produced as a belief and an ideology. People wear clothes believing that they are wearing fashion because it is something considered to be desirable. Clothing production involves the actual manufacturing of fabric and shaping it into a garment. The ideology of fashion needs to be sustained so that consumers return to purchase the items of clothing which are labeled as 'fashion.' The contents of fashion trends, that is particular items of clothing, may be abandoned and replaced with new styles, but the form of fashion remains and is always considered desirable in modern, industrialized nations.

6

Adoption and Consumption of Fashion

The sociological understanding of fashion involves an analysis of consumers who adopt fashion and their consumption behavior because the consumers participate indirectly in the production of fashion. When fashion reaches the stages of adoption and consumption, it is converted into something more concrete and visible, that is clothing-fashion. Once clothing is manufactured, it is worn and consumed. Once fashion is produced, it has also to be consumed in order for the belief to continue and perpetuate. Without the act of reception and consumption, the cultural product of fashion is not complete. Production influences consumption, and consumption influences production. Therefore, they can be treated simultaneously in the analysis of fashion. Similarly, the consumption aspect of cultural products must be taken into consideration, and we need to question how the consumers of fashion integrate with the producers of fashion. Fashion-ology involves the study of the social context in which fashion is not only produced but also consumed, and the meaning intended and assigned to the acts and settings of production and consumption. Cultural products, such as fashion, paintings and food, must be evaluated and interpreted in terms of their audience. Back explains the transition from producer to consumer and their relationship as follows:

> the lengthy path from producer to consumer is further continued by the intended audience. The consumer's arrangement of the final product, its composition, the occasion at which fashions are worn and displayed, become themselves creative occasions. Cultural creativity is continued in this way in the general public. This last step may be socially important in the use and development of fashions as the original production link. (1985: 3–4)

Thus, consumption cannot be considered in isolation. Fashion-ology consists of a sociology of fashion production as well as a sociology of fashion consumption because consumption and production are complementary, especially in today's diverse and complex fashion systems which include fashions emerging from youth culture. In this chapter, consumption will be reviewed from a historical perspective, and the connection between consumption as status and symbolic strategy, and the breakdown between consumption and production will be examined.

Consumption: A Historical Perspective

The model of modern-day consumption originated in pre-revolutionary court life, especially that of Louis XIV of France (1638–1715) who was known as 'the consumer king.' He indulged himself in lavish and opulent clothing and ornamentation. Handmade carpets, upholstery and curtains were changed every season at Versailles. Louis XIV is remembered for his sumptuous style of life rather than the important military, religious, or political events during his reign. There was the closed world of courtly consumption, and it was the court of Louis XIV that had made elegance and France synonymous (De Marly 1987). The purpose of such luxury was not to give pleasure either to the king or to his courtiers. It was an expression of his political power. Mukerji explains how serious he was in making France the center of aesthetic culture:

> For Louis XIV and his ministers, who took French claims to greatness more than seriously, having both the Great Tradition and trends in fashion located so firmly in Italy was unacceptable. If the French state was to become a center of European civilization, not just power, it had to take cultural leadership. So, Louis XIV followed classical precedent and had his achievements monumentalized through artworks, while Colbert manipulated fashion to make French goods desirable to elite consumers throughout Europe. Material beauty was more a matter of power and glory than an aesthetic issue to these men. (1997: 101)

The ceremonies of consumption, the feasts and fêtes, the balls and practices, were all part of a calculated system that had as its aim not individual gratification but enhancement of political authority. The consumer class was restricted to the courtly circle. The sixteenth-century aristocracy was nearly homogeneous in its consumer tastes because the ladies and gentlemen of the court acknowledged the king as the taste maker and the trendsetter. Williams explains the destructive spending behavior within the closed court culture:

Once admitted to the charmed circle of the court, however, a noble had to spend ruinously to stay there. He needed clothes embroidered with gold and silver threads and brilliant jewels to wear to the balls; a stable of horses and kennel of dogs for hunting; carriages with velvet upholstery and painted panels so that he could accompany the king on migrations to other palaces; houses and furnishings so that he could provide dances and dinners for the court; and dozens of valets and servants and stablehand, to all the rest possible. With rare exceptions, courtiers ran up stupendous debts. Although compelled by overwhelming pressure to perpetual imitation of the royal lifestyle, they had nothing like the king's income. (1982: 28–9)

Therefore, the history of France illustrates the nature and dilemmas of modern consumption. By the eighteenth century the way of life enjoyed by the French aristocracy and wealthy bourgeoisie had established itself as a prototype admired and imitated by upper classes throughout Europe.

This courtly style of consumption no longer exists but the life of consumers is more vigorous than ever. There is an incessant desire to purchase and consume, and those pleasures and feelings are available to ordinary people. Thus one homogeneous consumer style derived from a single source of authority shifted to a diversity of styles based on a multiplicity of authorities.

Consumer Revolution

Goods were obtained mainly through barter and self-production, so that the activity of consumption was closely linked with that of production. The consumption pattern then changed with the advent of mass consumption which came with mass production. A clear division was established between the activities of production and those of consumption. With industrial revolution came the consumer revolution which represented a change in tastes, preferences and buying habits. Williams explains how the consumers changed with the industrial revolution:

The industrial changes made possible large-scale production. The illusion of riches could be enjoyed in dress, especially in 'the democratization of the "silk dress," that ancient symbol of opulence, thus procuring the illusion of similarity in clothing – a great comfort for the feminine half of the human race.' . . . Technological advances had also transformed the feather industry: cheap and persuasive facsimiles of the rarest varieties, or even of totally imaginary ones, could be purchased by any shopgirl. Rabbit pelts could be turned into exotic furs like 'Mongolian chinchilla.' (1982: 97)

In the 1860s, the dress of peasant and also of working-class women was noticeably darker and cruder than the complicated trains, trailing skirts, laces and ribbons of wealthier women, but by the 1890s everyone wore shorter, simpler, more colorful clothes. Mass consumption means that similar merchandise reaches to all regions and all classes, and by the beginning of the twentieth century this uniform market was expanding in France and other parts of Europe. The consequences of this consumer revolution were numerous and diverse. First and foremost, people's value systems transformed. With mass production, fashion, which had been the epitome of luxury, was democratized, and consumption behavior began to change.

McCraken (1988) makes a comparison between patina and novelty to explain how and why fashion, which values newness, became acceptable. With the consumer revolution and the emergence of a consumer society, patina became less valued while novelty became highly valued and desirable. Patina used to serve as a kind of visual proof of status, and it suffered an eclipse in the eighteenth century (McCraken 1988: 32). There was a wide range of choices, and consumers were driven by new tastes and preferences. Society at large valued things that were new, which had more status than things that were old. Thus, fashion, whose essence is change, came to be highly important and meaningful. Furthermore, the rate of fashion change accelerated in the eighteenth century, and partly due to industrial development, what had once taken a year to change now took only a season. Marketers began to take advantage of the social as well as commercial dynamics of fashion and worked to increase its pitch. New techniques to create new styles and discredit old ones were constantly being developed. When a new fashion appeared, anyone with the necessary taste and resources could take possession of the latest innovation and use it for status purposes. This meant that first-generation wealth was now indistinguishable from the wealth of fifth-generation gentry (McCraken 1988: 40). As McKendrick remarks: 'Novelty became an irresistible drug for people in modern society' (1982: 10).

Like Blumer (1969a), who argued that fashion comes out of collective selection and that it is the consumers' taste that dictates fashion, McKendrick (1982) says that a change in productive means and ends cannot have occurred without a commensurate change in consumers' tastes and preferences. The English consumers welcomed the cheap calico and muslins imported from India in the 1690s (Mukerji 1983) because consumer tastes were changing, and that led to a new scale of domestic production and foreign imports. Due to eighteenth-century innovation and the commercialization of fashion, which made fashionable items more accessible, consumer demand changed. Industrial innovations included a more rapid obsolescence of style, the speedier diffusion of fashion knowledge, the appearance of marketing techniques such as the fashion doll and the fashion plate, the new and more active participation of previously excluded social groups, and new ideas about consumption and its contribution to the pubic good (McKendrick 1982).

Therefore, economic transformation and technological changes lowered the cost of existing consumer goods which made them readily available to all social classes. Steam engines made transportation more possible. The invention of printing and photography also had significant influence on mass consumption. Modern human beings have perpetual desire, and fashion seems to feed on it. As Williams says:

> The elitist consumer never finds a resting place, never attains an equilibrium, but must keep buying and discarding, picking up and dropping items, perpetually on the move to keep one jump ahead of the common heard. He therefore shares the fate of the mass consumer, who ... finds that illusions of wealth are always disappearing as once-unusual objects are sold in every department store and therefore lose their capacity to convey the aura of wealth. (1982: 139)

Miller (1981) examines the influence of the department store Bon Marché on the culture of nineteenth-century France and the important role it played in the consumer revolution. It provided not only a place to find and purchase goods but was organized to inflame people's material desires and feelings. The contribution of the department store to changing tastes and preferences, changing purchase behavior, a changing relationship between buyer and seller, and changing marketing techniques was immeasurable. It worked to shape and transfer cultural meaning of goods and also served as an important site for the conjunction of culture and consumption. The department store must be seen not only as a reflection of changing consumer patterns but also as a decisive agent which actively contributed to the culture in which consumption took place. The goods of the department store gave material expression to the values of the bourgeoisie and these objects, which had to be fashionable, made these values concrete and gave them a 'reality all their own' (Miller 1981: 180). Therefore, the department store materialized the values, attitudes and aspirations of the bourgeoisie. It infused goods with cultural meaning. Material symbols helped to reorganize the cultural meaning. Miller (1981) demonstrates how the large department stores became harbingers of the modern retailing world of today.

Consuming Fashion as Symbolic Strategy

Holbrook and Dixon (1985: 110) define fashion as public consumption through which people communicate to others the image they wish to project. This definition contains three primarily descriptive components: 1) public consumption, 2) communication to others, and 3) image.

First, by focusing on public consumption as the definition of fashion, the role of conspicuous usage that is open to inspection by others is stressed. Fashion behavior entails some display of one's preference hierarchy, some outward manifestation of inward evaluative judgments. In order for consumption to serve symbolically, it must be visible to others, which relates to Veblen's concept of conspicuous consumption. Material objects intentionally adopted for this purpose must be observable or noticeable. Fashion involves overt consumption behavior that makes one's tastes or values accessible to the awareness of others.

Second, communications with others through consumption became a signal to others as to which norms are shared and agreed upon agreement among a number of individuals. There has to be a consensus among people in society that a particular item of clothing is fashion. We do not call consumer behavior 'fashionable' if only one person does it. As noted in the previous chapters, fashion production as well consumption is a collective activity.

Third, image can be treated as a consumption system which involves complementarity. The nature of consumption patterns as symbol systems underlies the view of fashion as an attempt to communicate one's image. Image is a picture that one wishes to project to win approval, respect or prestige by appearing stylish, sophisticated or chic, and it functions within an interpersonal network system. Like any system, fashion involves not only added effects but also interactions among its parts. Thus one cannot treat fashion as the sum of isolated elements, but instead must consider the interrelations among its component parts. This approach is based on a structural-functionalist analysis. These components consist of complementary products so that fashion pertains not just to one product considered by itself, but rather to a number of products fitting together consistently to form a mutually reinforcing representation of the image one wishes to convey.

The cultural meaning of consumer goods is shifting. Meaning is constantly flowing to and from its several locations in the social world, aided by the collective and individual efforts of designers, producers, advertisers, and consumers. Contemporary culture has been associated with an increasingly materialistic or fetishistic attitude, and the symbolic dimension of consumption is increasingly becoming important. The value of fashion is the symbolic meaning, and fashionable merchandise must fill needs of the imagination and must be appealing to consumers. Fashion is the non-material dimension of modern culture. Fashion develops and is produced and reproduced continuously which results in a continuous public appetite for change; the producer offers novelties knowing that the consumer will probably accept them. Williams remarks:

> When they assume concrete form and masquerade as objective fact, dreams lose their liberating possibilities as alternatives to daylight reality. What is involved here is not a casual level of fantasy, a kind of mild and transient wishful thinking, but a far more thoroughgoing substitution of subjective images for external reality ... Imaginative desires and material ones, between dreams and commerce, between events of collective consciousness and of economic fact. (1982: 65)

While the audience of artworks consume art by watching them, the audience of fashion consumes fashion by wearing the clothes – unless they are displayed in a museum setting. This is the stage that is most crucial in the ideology of fashion because fashion as a belief is represented as a material object.

According to Bourdieu (1984), if there is a principle of organization to all forms of social life, it is the logic of distinction. In any differentiated society, individuals, groups, and social classes cannot escape this logic, and it brings them together while separating them from one another. The boundaries that we create are symbolic. Cultural consumption plays a central role in the process. Therefore, analyzing the different relations that people have with cultural objects helps us understand domination and subordination. Fashion can be used as a conceptual tool to understand the nature of symbolic activity.

Consumption and Social Status

In a society where there is a strong system of social stratification, objects tend to reflect given social hierarchies. In such society, sumptuary laws may be passed which forbid the use of particular goods by those who are deemed to be below a certain station in life (Braudel 1981; Mukerji 1983; Sennett 1976). The process of signification between material object and social position in this situation strives to remain rigid and controlled. However, when this breaks down, goods can change from being relatively static symbols to being more directly constitutive of social status. Under these conditions, emulation or imitation is increasingly significant and meaningful as a strategy by means of which people lower in a given social hierarchy attempt to realize their aspirations towards higher status, modifying their behavior, their dress and the kind of goods they purchase. Emulation in turn stimulates the desire to retain differentials, which often becomes based upon access to knowledge about goods and their prestige connotations. As a result, fashion emerges as the means for continuing those forms of social differentiation previously regulated by sumptuary rulings. In other words, demand for goods may flourish in the context of ambiguity in social hierarchy. Miller explains:

> What makes an object fashionable it is ability to signify the present; it is thus always doomed to become unfashionable with the movement of time. Fashion usually operates within a system of emulation and differentiation in knowledge, such that it uses the dynamic force of object change as a means of reinforcing the stability of the social system within which it is operating. (1987: 126)

There are two major classic studies that exemplify the significance of fashion consumption and the process of consumption: those of Simmel and Veblen. Simmel's analysis 1957([1904]) argues that fashion plays a major part in many people's attempts to live out the contradictory pulls of this perceived duality. Typically, Simmel does not present, a trend towards isolation and a trend towards integration as alternatives, but as necessarily contradictory elements of the same actions. Fashion demands an individual conception of conventional style, thereby allowing the preservation of a private world, a self-conception which is saved from exposure by the expediency of convention. In obeying the dictates of style, it is the social being which takes responsibility for choice, yet there is simultaneously an arena for personal strategy. Fashion then provides a surface which is partly expressive, but which also in part protects individuals from having to expose their taste in public. This study provides a clear exemplification of the concept of consumption activity as a means of living through necessary contradictions.

One can find the systemic implications of subordinate imitation. When low-standing individuals began to borrow high-standing status markers, high-standing individuals were forced to move on to new status markers. Every status marker could be imitated by lower social groups, and as a result, upper classes were forced to adopt new innovations in all product categories, including clothing. No sooner had the high-standing group moved to a new innovation than this, too, was appropriated by subordinate groups, and movement was required again. The fashion innovations they had adopted out of fancy, they now had to adopt out of necessity. With no patina strategy to protect them from fraudulent status claims, the only way of achieving such protection was to continually invent new fashions (McCraken 1988: 40).

On the other hand, Veblen's classic study of conspicuous consumption and status symbols created an analytical framework that has been the staple of sociological studies of consumer behavior. The basic premise of Veblen's discussion is similar to that of Simmel's, but it was Veblen who put the term 'conspicuous consumption' into general circulation. People acquire goods to compete with others. Fashion and clothing are used as symbols of social position and status. His theory explains the functions of fashion, which are clearly different from the functions of clothing – modesty and protection.

Veblen expressed the modes of pecuniary taste under three headings, conspicuous consumption, conspicuous waste and conspicuous leisure, and the three are all interrelated and are dependent on each other. Conspicuous consumption is for the purpose of impressing others and society at large, and the mere demonstration of purchasing power is the simplest device of fashion. Conspicuous waste is similar to conspicuous consumption. One can demonstrate one's superior wealth by giving away or destroying one's possessions. Conspicuous leisure is visible evidence that one is leading a life so far removed from all menial necessities that clothes can be worn which make any kind of physical labor difficult if not impossible. Dress of this kind, so long as it is manifestly sumptuous, marks the wearer as a member or a dependent of the leisure class: for instance, a sumptuous hat which gives no protection to the head, the great ruff around the neck of the early seventeenth century and long trailing sleeves which incapacitated arm and hand movements (Veblen 1957[1899]).

Veblen's theory of conspicuous consumption or competitive emulation is partly applicable today. We copy those of higher status with whom we are competing. People might also choose to copy someone they admire without considering his or her status. Such reverential emulation has the same result as the competitive, but the motivating factor is quite different. Being fashionable has to be something that is envied and desired; otherwise, the consumer would not adopt fashion nor wish to be fashionable. Indeed, fashion works as an expression of conspicuous consumption. Among more recent studies of consumption, Bourdieu (1984) offers a very similar analysis. He discusses the nature of cultural practices in industrial society, and he reduces almost all consumption to the play of social differentiation.

The trickle-down theory of fashion has several strengths. It places fashion diffusion in a social context and allows us to see how the movement of fashion articulates with the social system in which it takes place. However, Blumer (1969a) suggests that fashion must be seen as a process of 'collective selection' in which the trickle-down theory plays no significant part. Clothing does not take its prestige from the elite. Instead, 'potential fashionableness' (Blumer 1969a: 281) is determined by factors independent of the elite's control. Blumer argues that Simmel's theory, while suitable for European fashions in the past, cannot account for the fashion of modern society (1969a: 278).

Material goods transmit different messages about their owners, and it is the historian's job to decode these messages. Status seeking is only one aspect of 'the presentation of self' (Goffman 1959). Material culture provides the understanding of the symbolic properties that are attached to objects that humans manufacture. Material culture can carry status messages. Social scientists have sought to demonstrate how individuals and communities use inanimate objects to claim, to legitimate, and to compete for status meaning.

Consumers in Modern and Postmodern Times

Fashion information used to come mainly from one source: Paris. Consumers throughout the world who were fashion conscious emulated the French style, which epitomized and legitimated the most aesthetic appearance. Historically, fashionable clothing was consumed by those of high social standing and those with substantial fortune who could afford to indulge themselves in both a luxurious lifestyle and extravagant clothing. In the days when consumers were less fashion-conscious, designers and manufacturers tried to influence or even manipulate the public, though the public could, and often did, refuse to accept their suggested style changes. Today, the industry as a whole cannot impose fashion change, and no one individual designer can impose a radical change in style. It is not only the rich or upper classes who are consumers of fashion. Fashion is not confined to those who consider themselves socially or financially superior to the masses. Williams explains: 'French society lost a clearly defined group at its summit to establish a model of consumption, just as that group had lost one supreme individual to direct its taste. The social terrain was leveling out. Instead of looking upward to imitate a prestigious group people were more inclined to look at each other. Idolatry diminished; rivalry increased' (1982: 56).

Social scientists agree that Western societies have changed in the past decades, and people's patterns of consumptions are changing. As Millerson indicates, consumer behavior has been going through a major transition for the past decades: 'The mass market from the 1950s, 1960s and even the 1970s has disappeared, replaced by a phenomenon futurists and demographers call "demassification"; many different market segments, some moving over the speed limit, some at the speed limit, others chugging along as they always have, and still others struggling to stay on the highway' (1985: 99). Fashionable consumers impatiently wait to see what the fashion will be for the next season. Rogers (1983) classifies consumers into five different types based on how soon they adopt fashionable items: innovators, early adopters, early majority, late majority and laggards.

A Shift from Class Fashion to Consumer Fashion

In postmodern cultures, consumption is conceptualized as a form of role playing, as consumers seek to project conceptions of identity that are continually evolving. Social class is less evident and important in one's self-image and identity in contemporary society than before. Style differentiation no longer distinguishes social classes. There is a great deal of interclass and intra-class mobility. Social identity that used to be based on the economic and political spheres is now based on something outside. Crane remarks (2000: 11): 'the consumption of cultural goods, such as fashionable clothing, performs an increasingly important role in the construction of personal identity, while the satisfaction of material needs and the emulation of superior classes are secondary.' One's style of dress conveys an initial and continuing impression-making image. The variety of lifestyles available in contemporary society liberates the individual from tradition and enables him or her to make choices that create a meaningful self-identity (Giddens 1991). According to Crane:

> Clothing itself is less important than the frames that are used to sell it, which can be used in turn to sell licensed products. Consumers are no longer perceived as 'cultural dopes' or 'fashion victims' who imitate fashion leaders but as people selecting styles on the basis of their perceptions of their own identities and lifestyles. Fashion is presented as a choice rather than a mandate. The consumer is expected to 'construct' an individualized appearance from a variety of options. An amalgam of materials drawn from many different sources, clothing styles have different meanings for different social groups. (2000: 15)

As the structure of society has begun to change, and with the advent of technology, fashion information has spread from various sources through the multiple media at an amazingly fast pace. Instead of looking for the fashionable items of the season in Paris, consumers look elsewhere, and sometimes youth cultures create their own styles with their own definitions of fashions. I would call this another type of fashion system. The sources of fashion are becoming diverse, and a growing number of younger designers worldwide are emerging out of street culture and designing distinct street fashion. Nonetheless, there are still gatekeepers who make such designs fashion. Even street fashion must go through the process of admission to earn public recognition.

Breaking Production and Consumption Boundaries

An object is manufactured before it is purchased, and we therefore have a tendency to see consumption activities as the result of, or as a process secondary to, the development of manufacturing and other forms of production. However, in postmodern culture, the boundary is starting to collapse. For Becker (1982), there is no distinction between production and consumption in art worlds. The audiences are undistinguished from the artists. Everyone participates in producing and distributing their works. Becker discusses the socially constructed nature of art, and how it is valued. His approach incorporates the intention of demystifying art. He is against the mythology of artistic reputation. His approach comes from the phenomenological foundations of symbolic interactionism, a theoretical framework used in Fashion-ology. Becker starts with the assumption that, as in all social fields, it is in the regularized interactions among creators and their supporting personnel that social meanings arise. All become participants in the creative process, and production and reception merge. We learn a great deal from Becker about how artists live and work within the constraints of institutions which Fashion-ology seeks to identify.

The distinction between popular and high culture often appears in studying culture and the arts, and this may extend to the classification of high fashion and popular fashion. DiMaggio (1992) showed in his study that at the beginning of the twentieth century in the US, a high culture model was established in the visual by a distinct organizational system. He analyzed how differences in various categories were cultivated and institu- tionalized over time in order to maintain the distinctions. However, Crane (2000) argues that the high/low distinction is becoming arbitrary, and thus, we have to define cultures in terms of the environments in which they are created, produced and disseminated rather than in terms of content.

As consumers become increasingly fashionable and fashion conscious in modern and postmodern societies, they themselves become producers. Fashion was originally defined as dressing up, but the concept of dressing down began to emerge in democratic societies as class boundaries became less rigid. Street fashion first began as anti-fashion, but ironically it was acknowledged as fashion. This is the trickle-up theory of fashion.

As fashion defines the legitimate taste of clothing, people strive to find what that is, and this legitimate taste, according to Bourdieu (1984), is class-based, differing from one social class to another. However, in modern society, fashionable styles are provided in different forms for people in different social classes so that fashionable items can reach almost every level of consumer.

The punk fashion exemplifies the boundary disappearance between production and consumption of fashion. Punk first manifested itself among groups of unemployed young people and students in London in 1976. Punk culture seems to have developed as a reaction to unemployment and the general pessimism of youth. Punk was an anarchic, nihilistic style which deliberately set out to shock society. Punk clothing was almost entirely black and consciously menacing; it was often homemade or bought from secondhand thrift shops. Garments were frequently slashed and worn in disheveled layers. Both males and females shaved their heads, mutilated themselves and wore dirty and torn clothes. They used make-up and hair products to produce outrageous punk styles. Mendes and de la Haye describe styles that shaped punk identity as follows:

> Clothes for both sexes included tight black trousers teamed with mohair sweaters, leather jackets customized with paint, chains and metal studs. For female punks, miniskirts, black fishnet tights and stiletto-heeled shoes, and for both sexes bondage trousers joined with straps from knee to knee. Jackets and T-shirts often featured obscene or disturbing words or images. Garments were festooned with chains, zips, safety-pins and razor blades. Hair was dyed in different colors, and shaved and gelled to create Mohican spikes, makeup . . . blacken eyelids and lips. Multiples earring were popular, some also pierced their cheeks and noses. It also challenged both masculine stereotypes and long-held ideals of feminine beauty. (1999: 222)

Punks violated any conventions and norms that society forced upon them, and their challenging message attracted a large audience. It gave a sense of belonging to youngsters who were in search of an identity. As Hebdige explains:

> Amongst kids, this desire for coherence is particularly acute. Subculture provides a way of handling the experience of ambiguity and contradictions, the painful questions of identity. Each subculture provides its members with style, an imaginary coherence, a clear-cut ready-made identity which coalesces around certain chosen objects (a safety pin, a pair of winkle-pickers, a two-tone mohair suit). Together, these chosen objects

form a whole?a recognisable aesthetic which in turn stands for a whole set of values and attitudes. (1979: 23)

If a style is acknowledged by large numbers of people, it can become fashion. Punk fashion was conspicuous, but it was not an expression of conspicuous waste or leisure. Yet, it became fashion. Those styles began to be commercialized, and were filtered into mass-market fashion and even high fashion. They had a tremendous effect on British fashion, and designers, such as Zandra Rhodes, Vivienne Westwood and Malcolm McLaren, incorporated punk styles in their collections. Although punk fashion, which helped establish London's reputation for innovative youth style, was primarily associated with Britain, similar developments have taken shape in other parts of Europe, Japan and New York (Mendes and de la Haye 1999: 220). For instance, young Japanese designers are taking ideas from the streets of Tokyo and are extremely popular among teenagers who are trying to achieve a group identity. These designers constitute a new fashion system which is gradually being institutionalized as small independent and marginal labels known as the Indies fashion brands in order to separate themselves from the mainstream world-famous Japanese designers, such as Issey Miyake and Yohji Yamamoto. However, even street fashion needs to be diffused and to be legitimated as fashion.

Social Visibility of Fashion

In dealing with fashion consumption, we have to consider the group mentality of those who adopt and wear fashion. Mass fashion diffusion and consumption can be explained as a process of collective behavior among large numbers of people. They believe that whatever they are wearing is fashion. According to Lang and Lang (1961: 323), the fashion process is an elementary form of collective behavior, whose compelling power lies in the implicit judgment of an anonymous multitude. Individuals perceive societal clothing norms on television, in magazines, in movies, and on the streets of cities and evaluate their own fashion adoption in the light of these perceptions.

Fashion can be analyzed as a process of collective selection of a few styles from numerous competing alternatives. Innovative consumers may experiment with many possible alternatives, but the ultimate test in the fashion process is the competition between alternative styles for positions of 'fashionability.' Consumers try to discover the items of clothing which are defined as fashionable.

The increasing social visibility of a new style is the key to collective behavior in fashion. Mass fashion marketing and mass communication of information on new styles tend to homogenize and standardize consumer tastes, because the styles manufactured and promoted often resemble one another, even when many different manufacturers and retailers are involved in the fashion business. When a style is defined as fashionable, the apparel industries make copies of that style. The media and fashion advertisements or editorials in particular also confer social status and prestige on new fashions, building their social desirability and encouraging consumers to accept them. There is a tremendous amount of social visibility and a constant urge to be different from others, but not too different, only slightly different.

Conclusion

In modern and postmodern societies, consumption and production are complementary and, therefore, production does not take place within a completely separate sphere in relation to the broader social context of consumption. The relationship between production and consumption in the particular culture industry called fashion have been explored. Both empirical research and theoretical understanding are equally important and related through the ways in which products are circulated and given particular meanings through the range of production–consumption relationships. The meaning-making processes and practices do not simply arise out of one autonomous sphere of production but also out of consumption. Distinctions and differences between fashion and anti-fashion, high fashion and mass fashion, men and women, and rich and poor, among many other social categories, are breaking down.

7

Conclusion

This book has provided a different approach to fashion and has attempted to show how individuals and institutions within a fashion system interact with one another, how the designers, fashion professionals and consumers play their role, and how together they make fashion happen and sustain the culture of fashion. The effect of social structure upon participants and their influence on the social structure can be observed. Fashion-ology deals not only with individuals but with the social institutions of the fashion world and their effects upon the social and economic status of many individuals when fashion is used as a symbolic strategy. Contents and styles of clothing can be discussed in their relation to structural changes in the fashion system and, thus, they cannot be taken out of the social context.

Historically, fashion came out of Paris, and that was the center for the most aesthetic clothing. Fashion that used to be the privilege of the upper class is now enjoyed by almost everyone at every social level due to the democratization of fashion that was helped by mass production during the Industrial Revolution.

The emergence of avant-garde designers, such as the Japanese designers in the 1980s, was said to be the beginning of the postmodern phenomenon in the field of fashion, which allows openness to a great variety of styles and genres. The acceptance of these Asian outsider designers was interpreted as the breakdown of the racial boundaries among designers who were predominantly white. Postmodernity allows ethnic minorities, women, lesbians and gay men to assert, find or retrieve an identity (Wilson 1994). The definition of what is fashionable was gradually evaporating with the beginning of postmodernism which eliminated distinctions and with the demise of the autonomous sphere of fine art. What was worn as an underwear could be worn as outerwear. What used to be a hole for the neck could be worn as an armhole. Contents of fashions have become diverse and have redefined themselves implying the breakdown of the clothing system, that is, of sartorial conventions (Kawamura 2004). Postmodern, deconstructionist designers who have been greatly influenced by the Japanese, such as Ann Demeulemeester, Dries Van Noten and

Martin Margiela, have followed the trend. Like the Japanese, these Belgian designers from Antwerp have destroyed the normative clothing conventions found in the Western clothing system. The avant-garde has become so popular that it has changed the definition of what is beautiful, which is often synonymous with what is fashionable. The prototype of the fashion system in Paris is expanding its boundaries because it has been challenged by other fashion systems worldwide, such as those in London, New York, Milan, Tokyo and Sydney. The system needs to accept new designers to sustain various institutions of fashion, and new designers, in turn, need the system's recognition for their reputation.

Designers always emerged from fashion collections, but they are now coming out of the streets of London, Tokyo and other cities. The production of fashion used to be in the hands of the French system, but it is becoming difficult to distinguish production and consumption, and both are occurring elsewhere. For consumers in postmodern societies, anything and everything can be fashion. Any item of the clothing has the possibility of becoming a fashion. The source of legitimation that came from hegemonic Paris and the French establishment is, therefore, is losing its power. Youth culture is the epitome of the postmodern consumer as well as producer of fashion. Streets are treated as fashion laboratories, and they are replacing Haute Couture. Young people experiment with every possible clothing combination and create their own definitions of what fashion is. Fashion magazine institutions that diffused fashion from seasonal fashion collections mainly in Paris are going through a transition. New types of street fashion magazine are emerging around the world and are replacing mainstream fashion magazines that featured only the famous brand names.

Fashion now takes part in the cultural globalization. Globalization is about mobility across frontiers and also mobility of goods and commodities. It is also about the dissolution of the old structure and boundaries. In fashion, it is about the increasing transnationalization of designers coming from all over the world to Paris and also moving within the fashion systems. Fashion is global in the sense that Western or French clothes no longer define what is fashionable and beautiful. The next important question that Fashion-ology needs to pose is: to what extent can we expect the fashion systems to become more global, hybrid and decentralized?

$\mathcal{N}otes$

Chapter 1 Introduction

1. Institution is the term widely used to describe social practices that are regularly and continuously repeated, are sanctioned and maintained by social norms, and have a major significance in the social structure. The term refers to established patterns of behavior and is regarded as a general unit that incorporates a plurality of roles. Five types of major institution are conventionally identified: 1) economic, 2) political, 3) stratification, 4) familial and marital and 5) cultural, concerned with religious, scientific and artistic activities. Institutionalization is the process whereby social practices become sufficiently regular and continuous to be described as institutions. The notion indicates that changes in social practices both modify existing institutions and create new forms (Eisenstadt 1968: 409).

2. Sociological discourse and empirical studies of fashion will be discussed in detail in Chapter 2.

3. Translation: *The Dictionary of Twentieth-Century Fashion*

4. Craik 1994; Finkelstein 1996; Gaines and Herzog 1990; Hollander 1993; Kunzle 1982.

5. This will be elaborated in Chapter 6 of this book.

6. The term 'false consciousness' is used by Marxists to describe the situation where the proletariat fails to perceive what they believe to be the 'true' nature of its interests and does not develop a revolutionary class consciousness.

7. For women's styles in the 1920s and 1930s, see Baudot (1999), De Marly (1980a), Deslandres and Müller (1986), Grumbach (1993) and Laver (1995[1969]).

Chapter 3 Fashion as an Institutionalized System

1. The prototype of the fashion trade organization is found in Paris. It is called La Fédération de la Couture, du Prêt-à-Porter des Couturiers et des Créateurs de Mode (translated as The French Federation of Couture and Ready-to-Wear for Couturiers and Creators of Fashion).

2. Alison Lurie is a Pulitzer Prize winning novelist whose book *The Language of Clothes* (1981) has been widely quoted by fashion writers.

3. The details are in Yuniya Kawamura (2004).

Chapter 4 Designers: The Personification of Fashion

1. Max Weber describes three types of authority: traditional, legal–rational and charismatic. Charismatic authority first came to prominence in Weber's analysis of domination. Contrasted with legal-rational authority, charismatic authority is the authority vested in a leader by disciples and followers with the belief that the leader's claim to power flows from extraordinary personal gifts. With the death of the leader, the disciples either disband or convert charismatic beliefs and practices into traditional of legal arrangements. Charismatic authority is, therefore, unstable and temporary (Weber 1947).

2. Empire style dresses have a raised waistline with a horizontal seam below the bustline, and they have a slender silhouette.

3. The belle époque is a period of high artistic or cultural development, especially in France, at the beginning of the twentieth century.

4. A similar phenomenon can be found among Japanese designers in Paris (Kawamura 2004). Several designers who had worked with or under Issey Miyake, Yohji Yamamoto, Rei Kawakubo and Tokio Kumagai, such as Atsuro Tayama, Gomme, Junya Watanabe and Yoshiki Hishinuma, have now set up their own brands. There is an informal network among the Japanese designers in Paris.

Chapter 5 Production, Gatekeeping and Diffusion of Fashion

1. The term 'gatekeeper' or 'gatekeeping' has been applied in relation to judgments about admitting a person or works into a cultural field (Peterson 1994). Gatekeeping is a way in which affirmations, reinterpretations and rejections shape individual works and whole careers (Powell 1978).

2. Until 1850, the dolls were most often executed in wax, wood or cloth. After 1850 papíer-mâché was used, allowing for more detail in head styles.

3. Toile is a mock-up of a garment made out of plain and simple twill weave cotton or linen fabric.

Bibliography

Anspach, Karlyne (1967), *The Why of Fashion*, Ames, Iowa: Iowa State University Press.

Aspers, Patrik (2001), *Markets in Fashion: A Phenomenological Approach*, Stockholm: City University Press.

Back, Kurt W. (1985), 'Modernism and Fashion: A Social Psychological Interpretation,' in Michael R. Solomon (ed.), *The Psychology of Fashion*, Lexington, MA: Lexington Books.

Balzac, Honoré de (1830), *Traité de la vie élégante*, Paris: Bibliopoli.

Barnard, Malcolm (1996), *Fashion as Communication*, London: Routledge.

Barnhart, Robert K (1988),*The Barnhart Dictionary of Etymology*, New York: The H.W. Wilson Company.

Barthes, Roland (1964), *Elements of Semiology*, translated by A. Lavers and C. Smith, New York: Hill and Wang.

—— (1967), *The Fashion System*, translated by M. Ward and R. Howard, New York: Hill and Wang.

Bastide, Roger (1997), *Art et Société*, Paris: L'Harmattan.

Baudelaire, Charles (1964), *The Painter of Modern Life and Other Essays*, translated by Jonathan Mayne, London: Phaidon Press.

Baudot, Francois (1999), *Fashion: The Twentieth Century*, New York: Universe.

Baudrillard, Jean (1981), *For a Critique of the Political Economy of the Sign*, translated by Charles Levin, St Louis, MO: Telos Press.

—— (1993[1976]), *Symbolic Exchange and Death*, translated by E. Hamilton Grant, London: Sage Publications.

Becker, Howard S. (1982), *Art Worlds*, Berkeley: University of California Press.

Bell, Quentin (1976[1947]), *On Human Finery*, London: Hogarth Press.

Benedict, Ruth (1931), 'Dress', *Encyclopedia of the Social Sciences*, V, 235–7, London: Macmillan.

Bertin, Célia (1956), *Haute couture: terre inconnue*, Paris: Hachette.

Blumer, Herbert (1969a), 'Fashion: From Class Differentiation to Collective Selection,' *The Sociological Quarterly*, 10, 3: 275–91.

—— (1969b), *Symbolic Interactionism: Perspective and Method*, Englewoods Cliffs, NJ: Prentice-Hall.

Boucher, François (1987[1967]), *20,000 years of Fashion*, New York: H.N. Abrams.

Bourdieu, Pierre (1980), 'Haute couture et haute culture,' in *Questions de sociologies*, Paris: Les Editions de Minuit.

—— (1984), *Distinction: A Social Critique of the Judgment of Taste*, translated by R. Nice, Cambridge: Harvard University Press.

—— and Yvette Delsaut (1975), 'Le couturier et sa griffe,' *Actes de la recherche en sciences sociales*, 1, January: 7–36.

Braudel, Ferdinand (1981*)*, *The Structures of Everyday Life*, Chicago: University of Chicago Press.

Brenninkmeyer, Ingrid (1963), *The Sociology of Fashion*, Koln-Opladen: Westdeutscher Verlag.

Breward, Christopher (1995), *The Culture of Fashion*, Manchester: Manchester University Press.

Brewer, John and Roy Porter (eds) (1993), *Consumption and the World of Goods*, London: Routledge.

Brownmiller, Susan (1984), *Femininity*, New York: Linden Press/Simon & Schuster.

Burke, Peter (1993), '*Res et Verba*: Conspicuous Consumption in The Early Modern World,' in John Brewer and Roy Porter (eds), *Consumption and the World of Goods*. London: Routledge, 148–61.

Cannon, Aubrey (1998), 'The Cultural and Historical Contexts of Fashion,' in Sandra Niessen and Anne Bryden (eds) *Consuming Fashion: Adorning the Transnational Body* Oxford: Berg: 23–38.

Carlyle, Thomas (1831), *Sartor Resartus*, Oxford: Oxford University Press.

Clark, Terry N. (ed.) (1969), *Gabriel Tarde: On Communication and Social Influence*, Chicago: University of Chicago Press.

Coffin, Judith (1996), *The Politics of Women's Work: The Paris Garment Trades 1750–1915*, Princeton, NJ: Princeton University Press.

Coser, Lewis (1982), *Books: The Culture and Commerce of Publishing*, New York: Basic Books.

Craik, Jennifer (1994), *The Face of Fashion*, London: Routledge.

Crane, Diana (1987), *The Transformation of the Avant-Garde: The New York Art World 1940–1985*, Chicago: University of Chicago Press.

—— (1992), 'High Culture versus Popular Culture Revisited,' in Michèle Lamont and Marcel Fournier (eds), *Cultivating Differences: Symbolic Boundaries and the Making of Inequality*, Chicago: University of Chicago Press, 58–73.

—— (1993), 'Fashion Design as an Occupation,' *Current Research on Occupations and Professions*, 8: 55–73.

—— (1994), 'Introduction: The Challenge of the Sociology of Culture to Sociology as a Discipline,' in *The Sociology of Culture*, Oxford: Blackwell.

—— (1997a), 'Globalization, Organizational size, and Innovation in the French Luxury Fashion Industry: Production of Culture Theory Revisited,' *Poetics*, 24: 393–414.

—— (1997b), 'Postmodernism and the Avant-Garde: Stylistic Change in Fashion Design,' *MODERNISM/modernity*, 4: 123–40.

—— (1999), 'Diffusion Models and Fashion: A Reassessment, in The Social Diffusion of Ideas and Things,' *The Annals of The Academy of Political and Social Science*, 566, November: 13–24.

—— (2000), *Fashion and its Social Agendas: Class, Gender, and Identity in Clothing*, Chicago: University of Chicago Press.

Crowston, Clare Haru (2001), *Fabricating Women: The Seamstresses of Old Regime France, 1675–1791*, Durham, NC: Duke University Press.

Dalby, Liza (1993), *Kimono: Fashioning Culture*, New Haven, CT: Yale University Press.

Davenport, Millia (1952), *A History of Costume*, London: Thames and Hudson.

Davis, Fred (1985), 'Clothing and Fashion as Communication,' in Michael R. Solomon (ed.), *The Psychology of Fashion*, Lexington, MA: Lexington Books.

—— (1992), *Fashion, Culture, and Identity*, Chicago: University of Chicago Press.

De la Haye, Amy and Shelley Tobin (eds) (1994), *Chanel: The Couturière at Work*, Woodstock, NewY: Overlook Press.

De Marly, Diana (1980a), *The History of Haute Couture: 1850–1950*, New York: Holmes and Meier.

—— (1980b), *Worth: Father of Haute Couture*, New York: Holmes and Meier.

—— (1987), *Louis XIV & Versailles*, New York: Holmes and Meier.

—— (1990), *Christian Dior*, New York: Holmes and Meier.

Delbourg-Delphis, Marylène (1981), *Le chic et le look*, Paris: Hachette.

—— (1983), *La mode pour la vie*, Paris: Editions Autrement.

Delpierre, Madeleine (1997), *Dress in France in the Eighteenth Century*, translated by Caroline Beamish, New Haven, CT: Yale University Press.

Deslandres, Yvonne and Florence Müller (1986), *Histoire de la mode au XXe siècle*, Paris: Somology.

Dickie, George (1975), *Art and Aesthetics: An Institutional Analysis*, Ithaca, NY: Cornell University Press.

Diehl, Mary Ellen (1976), *How to Produce a Fashion Show*, New York: Fairchild Publications, Inc.

DiMaggio, Paul (1992), 'Cultural Entreneurship in 19th Century Boston,' in Michèle Lamont and Marcel Fournier (eds), *Cultivating Differences: Symbolic Boundaries and the Making of Inequality*, Chicago: University of Chicago Press.

—— and Michael Useem (1978), 'Cultural Democracy in a Period of Cultural Expansion: the Social Composition of Arts Audiences in the United States,' *Social Problems*, 26: 2.

Douglas, Mary and Baron Isherwood (1978), *The World of Goods: Towards an Anthropology of Consumption*, London: Routledge.

Duncan, Hugh Dalziel (1969), *Symbols and Social Theory*, Oxford: Oxford University Press.

Durkheim, Emile (1951[1897]), *Suicide*, translated by John Spaulding and George Simpson, New York: Free Press.

—— (1965[1912]), *The Elementary Forms of Religious Life*, New York: Free Press.

Eicher, Joanne B. (1969), *African Dress; A Selected and Annotated Bibliography of Subsaharan Countries*, African Studies Center: Michigan State University.

—— (1976), *Nigerian Handcrafted Textiles*, Ile-Ife: University of Ife Press.

—— (ed.) (1995), *Dress and Ethnicity: Change Across Space and Time*, Oxford: Berg.

—— and Ruth Barnes (1992), *Dress and Gender: Making and Meaning in Cultural Contexts*, Oxford : Berg.

—— and Mary Ellen Roach (eds) (1965), *Dress, Adornment, and the Social Order*, New York: Wiley.

—— and Lidia Sciama (1998), *Beads and Bead Makers: Gender, Material Culture, and Meaning*, Oxford: Berg.

Eisenstadt, S.N. (1968), 'Social Institutions: The Concept,' in D.L. Sils (ed.), *International Encyclopedia of the Social Sciences*, 14: 409–21, New York: Macmillan and Free Press.

Elias, Norbert (1983), *Court Society*, Oxford: Blackwell.

Entwistle, Joanne (2000), *The Fashioned Body: Fashion, Dress and Modern Social Theory*, Cambridge: Polity.

—— and Elizabeth Wilson (2001), *Body Dressing*, Oxford: Berg.

Fairchilds, Cissie (1993), 'The Production and Marketing of Populuxe Goods in Eighteenth-Century Paris,' in John Brewer and Roy Porter (eds), *Consumption and the World of Goods*, London: Routledge, 148–61.

Finkelstein, Joanne (1996), *After a Fashion*, Carlton: Melbourne University Press.

Flugel, J.C. (1930), *The Psychology of Clothes*, London: Hogarth.

Fraser, W. (1981), The Coming of the Mass Market, London: Macmillan.

Gaines, Jane and Jane Herzog (eds) (1990), *Fabrications: Costume and the Female Body*, London: Routledge.

Garfinkel, Stanley (1991), 'The Théâtre de la Mode: Birth and Rebirth,' in Susan Train and Eugène Clarence Braun-Munk (eds) *Le théâtre de la mode*, New York: Rizzoli International Publications, Inc.

Garland, Madge (1962), *Fashion: A Picture Guide to its Creators and Creation*, London: Penguin Books.

Gasc, Nadine (1991), 'Haute Couture and Fashion 1939–1946,' *Le Théâtre de la Mode*, New York: Rizzoli International Publications, Inc.

Gerth, H.H. and C. Wright Mills (1970*), From Max Weber: Essays in Sociology*, Oxford: Oxford University Press.

Giddens, Anthony (1991), *Modernity and Self-Identity: Self and Society in the Late Modern Age*, Cambridge: Polity.

Goblot, Edmond (1967[1925])), *La barrière et le niveau*, Paris: Librairie Félix Alcan.

Godard de Donville, Louise (1978), *Signification de la mode sous Louis XIII*, Aix-en-Provence: Edisud.

Goffman, Irving (1959), *The Presentation of Self in Everyday Life*, New York: Anchor Books.

Gramsci, Antonio (1975), *Antonio Gramsci: Further Selections from the Prison Notebooks*, edited and translated by Derek Bothman, London: Laurence and Wishart.

Green, Nancy (1997), *Reay-to-Wear and Ready-to-Work: A century of Industry and Immigrants in Paris and New York*, Durham, NC: Duke University Press.

Greenberg, Clement (1984), 'Complaints of an Art Critic,' in C. Harrison and F. Orton (eds), *Modernism, Criticism, Realism: Alternative Contexts for Art*, New York: Harper and Row.

Griswold, Wendy (2000), *Bearing Witness: Readers, Writers, and the Novel in Nigeria*, Princeton, NJ: Princeton University Press.

Grumbach, Didier (1993), *Histoires de la mode*, Paris: Editions du Seuil.

Hall, Richard H. (1999), *Organizations: Structures, Processes, and Outcomes*, New Jersey: Prentice Hall.

Hanser, Arnold (1968), *The Social History of Art*, vol. 2, London: Routledge.

Hebdige, Dick (1979), 'Putting on the Style,' *Time Out*, August 17.

Hénin, Janine (1990), *Paris Haute Couture*, Paris: Editions Philippe Olivier.

Hirsch, Paul (1972) 'Processing Fads and Fashions: An Organization Set Analysis of Cyltural Industry Systems,' in *American Journal of Sociology*, 77, January: 639–59.

Holbrook, Morris B. and Glenn Dixon (1985), 'Mapping the Market for Fashion: Complementarity in Consumer Preferences,' in Michael R. Solomon (ed.), *The Psychology of Fashion*, Lexington, MA: Lexington Books.

Hollander, Anne (1993), *Seeing Through Clothes*, Berkeley: University of California Press.

—— (1994), *Sex and Suits*, New York: Alfred A. Kopf.

Horn, Marilyn J. (1968), *The Second Skin*, Boston: Houghton Mifflin Co.

—— and Lois Gurel (1975), *The Second Skin*, Boston: Houghton-Mifflin.

Hunt, Alan (1996), *Governance of the Consuming Passions: A History of Sumptuary Law*, New York: St. Martin's Press.

Hunt, Lynn (1984), *Politics, Culture, and Class in the French Revolution*, Berkeley: University of California Press.

Hurlock, Elizabeth B. (1929), *The Psychology of Dress*, New York: The Ronald Press Company.

Katz, Elihu (1999), 'Theorizing Diffusion: Tarde and Sorokin Revisited,' *The Annals of The Academy of Political and Social Science*, 566, November: 144–55.

—— Martin Levin and Herbert Hamilton (1963), 'Traditions of Research on the Diffusion of Innovation,' *American Soiological Review*, 28: 237–52.

—— and Paul Lazarsfeld (1955), *Personal Influence*, New York: Free Press.

Kawamura, Yuniya (2001), 'The Legitimation of Fashion: Japanese Designers in the French Fashion System,' Columbia University, unpublished Ph.D. thesis.

—— (2004), *The Japanese Revolution in Paris Fashion*, Oxford: Berg.

Koenig, Rene (1973), *The Restless Image: A Sociology of Fashion*, translated by F. Bradley, London: George Allen & Unwin, Ltd.

Kroeber, A.L. (1919), *On the Principle of Order in Civilization as Exemplified by Changes in Fashion*, New York: Hill and Wang.

Kunzle, David (1982), *Fashion and Fetishism: A Social History of the Corest, Tight-Lacing and Other Forms of Body-Sculpture in the West*, Totowa, NJ: Rowman and Littlefield.

Lang, Kurt and Gladys Lang (1961), *Fashion: Identification and Differentiation in the Mass Society in Collective Dynamics*, New York: Thomas Y. Crowell Co.

Langner, Lawrence (1959), *The Importance of Wearing Clothes*, New York: Hastings House.

Laver, James (1950), *Dress*, London: Murray.

—— (1969), *Modesty in Dress*, London: Heinemann.

—— (1995[1969]), *Concise History of Costume and Fashion*, New York: H.N. Brams.

Le Bon, Gustave (1895), *The Crowd*, London: T. Fischer Unwin Ltd.

Le Bourhis, Katell (1991), 'American on its Own: The Fashion Context of the Theatre de la Mode in New York,' in Susan Train and Eugène Clarence Braun-Munk (eds) *Le thèâtre de la mode*, New York: Rizzoli International Publications, Inc.

Leopold, Ellen (1993), 'The Manufacture of the Fashion Ssytem,' in Juliet Ash and Elizabeth Wilson (eds), *Chic Thrills: A Fashion Reader*, Berkeley: University of California Press.

Lipovetsky, Gilles (1994), *The Empire of Fashion*, translated by Catherine Porter, Princeton, NJ: Princeton University Press.

Lopes, Paul and Mary Durfee (eds) (1999), 'The Social Diffusion of Ideas and Things,' *The Annals of The Academy of Political and Social Science*, 566, November.

Lurie, Alison (1981), *The Language of Clothes*, London: Bloomsbury.

Mallarmé Stephané (1933), *La Dernière Mode*, New York: The Institute of French Studies, Inc.

McCracken, Grant D. (1985), 'The Trickle-Down Theory Rehabilitated,' in Michael R. Solomon (ed.), *The Psychology of Fashion*, Lexington, MA: D.C. Heath Lexington Books.

—— (1987), 'Clothing as Language: An Object Lesson in the Study of the Expressive Properties of Material Culture,' in Barrie Reynolds and Margaret A. Scott (eds), *Material Anthropology: Contemporary Approaches to Material Culture*, Lanham, MD: University Press of America, Inc.

—— (1988), *Culture and Consumption: New Approaches to the Symbolic Character of Consumer Goods and Activities*, Bloomington, IN: Indiana University Press.

McDowell, Colin (1997), *Forties Fashion and the New Look*, London: Bloomsbury.

McKendrick, Neil (1982), *A Consumer Society: The Commercialization of Eighteenth-Century England*, London: Hutchinson.

——, John Brewer and J.H. Plumb (1982), *The Birth of a Consumer Society*, London: Europa.

Mendes, Valerie and Amy de la Haye (1999), *20th Century Fashion*, London: Thames & Hudson.

Menger, Pierre-Michel (1993), 'L'hégémonie parisienne: Economie et politique de la gravitation artistique,' *Annales ESC*, 6 November-December,: 1565–1600.

Menkes, Suzy (1996), 'Couture: Some Like it Haute, but Others are Going Demi,' *International Herald Tribune*, November 26: 11.

Merton, Robert (1957), *Social Theory and Social Structure*, New York: Free Press.

Milbank, Caroline Rennolds (1985), *Couture: Les grands Créateurs*, Paris: Robert Laffont.

Miller, Daniel (1987), *Material Culture and Mass Consumption*, Oxford: Blackwell.

Miller, Michael B. (1981), *The Bon Marché: Bourgeois Culture and the Department Store 1869–1920*, London: George Allen and Unwin.

Millerson, Jon S. (1985), 'Psychosocial Strategies for Fashion Advertising,' in Michael R. Solomon (ed.), *The Psychology of Fashion*, Lexington, MA: Lexington Books.

Monnier, Gérard (1995), *L'art et ses institutions en France: De la Révolution a nos jours*, Paris: Editions Galliard.

Moulin, Raymonde (1987), *The French Art Market: A Sociological View*, New Brunswick, NJ: Rutgers University Press.

Mukerji, Chandra (1983), *From Graven Images*, New York: Columbia University Press.

—— (1997), *Territorial Ambitions and the Gardens of Versailles*, Cambridge: Cambridge University Press.

Murray, James A.H. (ed.) (1901), *A New Oxford English Dictionary on Historical Principles*, Oxford: Clarendon Press.

Negus, Keith (1977). 'The Production of Culture,' in Paul du Gay (ed.), *Production of Culture/Culture of Productions*, London: Sage Publications.

Niessen, Sandra and Anne Brydon (1998), 'Introduction: Adorning the Body,' in Sandra Niessen and Anne Brydon (eds), *Consuming Fashion: Adorning the Transnational Body*, Oxford: Berg.

Nystrom, Paul H. (1928), *Economics of Fashion*, New York: The Ronald Press Company.

Oxford Thesarus American Edition, The (1992), Oxford: Oxford University Press.

Parsons, Talcott (1968), *The Structure of Social Action*, Volume I, New York: Free Press.

Perrot, Philippe (1994), *Fashioning the Bourgeoisie: A History of Clothing in the Nineteenth Century*, translated by Richard Bienvenu, Princeton, NJ: Princeton University Press.

Peterson, Richard A. (ed.) (1976), *The Production of Culture*, London: Sage Publications.

—— (1978), 'The Production of Cultural Change: The Case of Contemporary Country Music,' *Social Research*, 45: 2.

—— (1994), 'Culture Studies Through the Production Perspective: Progress and Prospects,' in Diana Crane (ed.), *The Sociology of Culture*, Oxford: Blackwell.

—— (1997), *Creating Country Music: Fabricating Authenticity*, Chicago: University of Chicago Press.

—— and David G. Berger (1975), 'Cycles in Symbol Production: The Case of Popular Music,' *American Sociological Review*, 40.

Polhemus, Ted (1994), *Street Style*, London: Thames and Hudson.

—— (1996), *Style Surfing*, London: Thames and Hudson.

—— and Lynn Proctor (1978), *Fashion and Antifashion: An Anthropology of Clothing and Adornment*, London: Thames and Hudson.

Powell, Walter (1972), *The New Institutionalism in Organizational Analysis*, Chicago: University of Chicago Press.

—— (1978), 'Publishers' Decision-Making: what Criteria do they Use in Deciding which Books to Publish?,' *Social Research*, 34, 2.

Random House Dictionary of the English Language, The (1987), New York: Random House.

Remaury, Bruno (ed.) (1996), *Dictionnaire de la mode au XXe siècle*, Paris: Editions du Regard.

—— and Nathalie Bailleux (1995), *Mode et Vêtements*, Paris: Gallimard.

Ribeiro, Aileen (1988), *Fashion in the French Revolution*, New York: Holmes and Meier.

—— (1995), *The Art of Dress: Fashion in England and France 1750 to 1820*, New Haven, CT: Yale University Press.

Roach-Higgins, Mary Ellen (1995), 'Awareness: Requisite to Fashion,' in Mary Ellen Roach-Higgins, Joanne B. Eicher and Kim K.P. Johnson (eds), *Dress and Identity*, New York: Fairchild Publications.

—— and Joanne Eicher (1973), *The Visible Self: Perspectives on Dress*, New Jersey: Prentice-Hall, Inc.

—— and Kathleen Ehle Musa (1980), *New Perspectives on the History of Western Dress*, New York: NutriGuides, Inc.

Roche, Daniel (1994), *The Culture of Clothing: Dress and Ffashion in the Ancien Regime*, translated by Jean Birrell, Cambridge: Cambridge University Press.

Rogers, Everett M. (1983), *Diffusion of Innovations*, New York: Free Press.

Ross, Edward A. (1908), *Social Psychology*, London: Macmillan.

Rossi, Ino (1983), *From the Sociology of Symbols to the Sociology of Signs*, New York: Columbia University Press.

Rouse, Elizabeth (1989), *Understanding Fashion*, London: BSP Professional Books.

Rousseau, Jean-Jacques (1750), *Discours sur les sciences et les arts*, Hanover: University Press of New England for Dartmouth College.

Ryan, John and Richard A. Peterson (1982), 'The Product Image: The Fate of Creativity in Country Music Songwriting,' in James S. Ettema and D. Charles Whitney (eds), *Individuals in Mass Media Organizations: Creativity and Constraint*, London: Sage Publications.

Ryan, John and William M. Wentworth (1999), *Media and Society: The Production of Culture in the Mass Media*, Boston: Allyn and Bacon.

Ryan, Mary S. (1966), *Clothing: A Study in Human Behavior*, New York: Holt, Rinehard & Winston.

Sahlins, Marshall (1976), *Culture and Practical Reason*, Chicago: University of Chicago Press.

Sapir, Edward (1931), 'Fashion,' *Encyclopedia of the Social Sciences*, Volume 6, London: Macmillan.

Sargentson, Carolyn (1996), *Merchants and Luxury Markets: The Marchands Merciers of Eighteenth-Century Paris*, London: Victoria and Albert Museum.

Saunders, Edith (1955), *The Age of Worth: Couturier to the Empress Eugenie*, Bloomington: Indiana University Press.

Saussure, Ferdinand de (1972), *Course in General Linguistics*, London: Fontana/Collins.

Sennett, Richard (1976), *The Fall of Public Man*, Cambridge: Cambridge University Press.

Simmel, Georg (1957[1904]), 'Fashion,' *The American Journal of Sociology*, LXII, 6, May: 541–58.

Skov, Lise (1996), 'Fashion Trends, Japonisme and Postmodernism,' *Theory, Culture and Society*, 13, 3, August: pp. 129–51.

—— (2003), 'A Japanese Globalization Experience and a Hong Kong Dilemma,' in Sandra Niessen, Anne Marie Leshkowich and Carla Jones (eds), *Re-Orienting Fashion*, Oxford: Berg.

Sombart, Werner (1967), *Luxury and Capitalism*, translated by W.R. Ditmar, Ann Arbor, MI: The University of Michigan Press.

Sorokin, Pitrim (1941), *Social and Cultural Mobility*, New York: Free Press.

Spencer, Herbert (1966[1896]), *The Principles of Sociology*, Volume II, New York: D. Aooleton and Co.

Sproles, George B. (1985), 'Behavioral Science Theories of Fashion,' in Michael R. Solomon (ed.) *The Psychology of Fashion*, Lexington, MA: D.C. Heath Lexington Books.

Stone, Gregory (1954), 'City Shoppers and Urban Identification: Observations on the Social Psychology of City Life,' *Amercian Journal of Sociology*, 60: 36–45.

Steele, Valerie (1985), *Fashion and Eroticism*, Oxford: Oxford University Press.

—— (1988), *Paris Fashion: A Cultural History*, Oxford: Oxford University Press.

—— (1991), *Women of Fashion: Twentieth-Century Designers*, New York: Rizzoli International Publications.

—— (1992), 'Chanel in Context,' in Juliet Ash and Elizabeth Wilson (eds), *Chic Thrills: A Fashion Reader*, Berkeley: University of California Press.

—— (1997), *Fifty Years of Fashion: New Look to Now*, New Haven, CT: Yale University Press.

—— and John S. Major (1999), *China Chic: East Meets West*, New Haven, CT: Yale University Press.

Sudjic, Deyan (1990), *Rei Kawakubo and Comme des Garçans*, New York: Rizzoli.

Sumner, William Graham (1940[1906]), *Folkways: A Study of the Sociological Importance of Usages, Manners, Customs, Mores and Morals*, Boston: Ginn and Company.

—— and Albert Gallway Keller (1927), *The Science of Society*, Volume 3, New Haven, CT: Yale University Press.

Szántó, András (1996), 'Gallery Transformation in the New York Art World in the 1980s', Columbia University, unpublished Ph.D. thesis.

Tarde, Gabriel (1903), *The Laws of Imitation*, translated by Elsie C. Parsons, New York: Henry Holt.

Taylor, Lou (1992), 'Paris Couture: 1940–1944,' in Juliet Ash and Elizabeth Wilson (eds), *Chic Thrills: A Fashion Reader*, Berkeley: University of California Press.

—— (2002), *The Study of Dress History*, Manchester: Manchester University Press.

Thomas, Chantal (1999), *The Wicked Queen: The Origins of the Myth of Marie-Antoinette*, New York: Zone Books.

Thornton, Nicole (1979), 'Introduction,' in *Poiret*, London: Academy Editions.

Tobin, Shelley (1994), 'The Foundations of the Chanel Empire,' in Amy de la Haye and Shelley Tobin (eds), *Chanel: The Couturière at Work*, Woodstock, NY: Overlook Press.

Toennies, Ferdinand (1961[1909]), *Custom: An Essay on Social Codes*, translated by A. F. Borenstein, New York: Free Press.

—— (1963[1887]), *Community and Society*, New York: Harper and Row.

Train, Susan and Eugène Clarence Braun-Munk (eds) (1991), *Le théâtre de la mode*, New York: Rizzoli International Publications, Inc.

Tseelon, Efrat (1994), 'Fashion and Signification in Baudrillard,' in *Baudrillard: A Critical Reader* , Oxford: Blackwell.

—— (1995),*The Masque of Femininity*, London: Sage Publications.

Veblen, Thorstein (1957[1899]), *The Theory of Leisure Class*, London: Allen and Unwin.

Veillon, Dominique (1990), *La mode sous l'Occupation*, Paris: Editions Payot.

Vernon, G.M. (1978), *Symbolic Aspects of Interaction*, Washington, D.C.: University Press of America.

Von Boehn, Max (1932), *Modes and Manners*, Volume 1, New York: Benjamin Blom.

Weber, Max (1947), *The Theory of Social and Economic Organization*, Oxford: Oxford University Press.

White, Harrison (1993), *Careers and Creativity: Social Forces in the Arts*, Boulder, CO: Westview Press.

—— and Cynthia White (1993[1965]), *Canvases and Careers: Institutional Change in the French Painting World*, New York: John Wiley.

Williams, Raymond (1981), *Culture*, Glasgow: Fontana.

Williams, Rosalind (1982), *Dream World: Mass Consumption in Late Nineteenth-Century France*, Berkeley: University of California Press.

Wilson, Elizabeth (1985), *Adorned in Dreams: Fashion and Modernity*, Berkeley: University of California Press.

—— (1994), 'Fashion and Postmodernism,' in John Storey (ed.), *Cultural Theory and Popular Culture*, New York: Harvester Wheatsheaf.

Wolff, Janet (1983), *Aesthetics and the Sociology of Art*, London: Allen & Unwin.

—— (1993),*The Social Production of Art*, New York: New York University Press.

Wollstonecraft, Mary (1792), *A Vindication of the Rights of Woman*, London: J. Johnson.

Worth, Gaston (1895), *La couture et la confection des vêtements de femme*, Boston: Little, Brown and Company.

Worth, Jean-Philippe (1928), *A Century of Fashion*, Translated by Ruth Scott Miller, Boston: Little, Brown and Company.

Young, Agatha Brooks (1966[1939]), *Recurring Cycles of Fashion: 1760–1937*, New York: Cooper Square Publishers.

Zeldin, Theodore (1977), *France 1848–1945*, Volume 2, Oxford: Oxford University Press.

Zolberg, Vera (1990), *Constructing a Sociology of the Arts*, Cambridge: Cambridge University Press.

—— (2000), 'African Legacies, American Realities: Art and Artists on the Edge,' in Vera Zolberg and Joni Maya Cherbo (eds), *Outsider Art: Contesting Boundaries in Contemporary Culture*, Cambridge: Cambridge University Press.

—— and Joni Maya Cherbo (eds) (2000), *Outsider Art: Contesting Boundaries in Contemporary Culture*, Cambridge: Cambridge University Press.

Index

manifest functions, 41
mannequin, 82, 83
Margiela, Martin, 106
marketers, 73, 92
McCracken, Grant, 46, 76, 78
Mendes, Valerie, 85
Merton, Robert, 86
micro-fashions, 49
milliner, 82, 83
Minagawa, Makiko, 64
Miyake, Issey, 60, 64
models, 83
modernity, 24–6
Montespan, Madame de, 76
Mukerji, Chandra, 90
Musa, Kathleen Ehle, 46
myth, 43

neophilia, 6
newness, 25
Niessen, Sandra, 8
Note, Dries Van, 105
novelty, 6, 33

Paris, 61, 85
patina, 92
pattern-makers, 51
Perrot, Philippe, 5, 25
Peterson, Richard, 33
photographers, 76
Poiret, Paul, 57, 67
Polhemus, Ted, 5, 58
Pompadour, Madame de, 76
postmodernity, 25
Prêt-à-Porter, 70
public opinion, 78
public relations, 45
publicists, 66
punk, 101

quantitative methods, 17–18
Queen of England, 83

Remaury, Bruno, 3
reputation, 57
Ribeiro, Aileen, 8, 11
Roach-Higgins, Mary Ellen, 13, 15, 51
Roche, Daniel, 5

sample cutters, 51
sample-makers, 51
sari, 51
semiotic analysis, 39
Simmel, Georg, 9, 13, 20, 22, 25, 29, 58, 71, 96
social capital, 54
social identity, 99
social mobility, 24–6
social science
  fashion in, 13–18
social structure, 42
sociological theory, 42
sociology of arts, 1
sociology of culture, 32–3
Spencer, Herbert, 13, 20, 21, 22
stars, 57
  in culture industries, 66–7
status, 48, 57, 61
Steele, Valerie, 10, 15, 16, 68, 71
stitching machinery, 86
stratification, 36
structural functionalism, 40
style, 3
Sudjic, Deyan, 63
Sumner, William Graham, 13, 20, 23
sumptuary laws, 24
symbolic capital, 54, 55
symbolic interactionism, 40, 42